# no cook cookbook

quadrille

# nocook cookbook

over 200 simple
recipes and ideas
for mouthwatering
meals without cooking

## Orlando Murrin    photography by Jason Lowe

to Peter

Editorial director: **Jane O'Shea**  Art director: **Mary Evans**

Editor & project manager: **Lewis Esson**  Photography: **Jason Lowe**

Home economist: **Jane Suthering**  Production: **Beverley Richardson**

First published in 2003 by Quadrille Publishing Limited,
Alhambra House, 27-31 Charing Cross Road, London WC2H OLS

Text © Orlando Murrin 2003  Photography © Jason Lowe 2003
Design & layout © Quadrille Publishing Ltd 2003

The rights of Orlando Murrin to be identified as the Author of this
Work have been asserted by him in accordance with the Copyright,
Design and Patents Act 1988.

Cataloguing in Publication Data: a catalogue record for this book is
available from the British Library

ISBN 1 84400 028 1   Printed in China through World Print Ltd

**contents**

no-cooking is easy... you don't need
any specialist equipment and you
don't have to master difficult
techniques. It's all a question of choosing
the best quality ingredients and
treating them sympathetically

# no-cook
# guidelines

To get you off to a good start, overleaf you'll
find some helpful lists of those ingredients that
I really find are a boon to the no-cook. At the
end of the book (page 158) you'll also find a
comprehensive list of those things that
I recommend you keep in your storecupboard
to help make no-cooking even easier. Generally,
these are the items that I list in the recipe
ingredients under the heading 'Make sure
you've got'. While 'What you need' lists those
items I think you are probably going to have to
buy in specially for the dish in question.

    You will see that the three concessions to
cooking that I allow myself are boiling water in
a kettle and melting chocolate and butter.

    Happy no-cooking!

# no-cook refrigerator & freezer requisites

herbs as they magically brighten flavours and turn ordinary ingredients into something special. Fresh coriander gives a hint of the exotic; basil and tarragon the Med; chives make things lip-lickingly tasty; parsley freshens.

tomatoes because they are luscious, juicy and taste of the sun. I usually halve them and squeeze out the pulp and seeds, as this makes them sweeter and tastier. Always choose cherry or vine-ripened tomatoes.

lemons and limes as they add a fresh, piquant note. Use grated lemon zest to give a zing. Go easy on the juice – it's often better to squeeze it over the finished dish than risk mixing it in. A flick of lime zest transports you instantly to the tropics.

cheeses because there's a different type for every occasion. Keep a supply of jars of goats' cheese and feta in oil, bagged mozzarella for salads, hard cheeses for grating.

seafood as fresh prawns, smoked salmon and Avruga (herring) caviar spell instant luxury. Smoked salmon is a feast in itself, or can be conjured into snacks or salads.

spring onions as they add instant pizzazz. I invariably shred them – trim, leaving a bit of green, then chop thinly at a sharp angle. Red spring onions add colour.

celery and cucumber for their crunch. If you can find white celery it tastes better, but always cut it finely. Cucumber can be used peeled or not. I usually first cut it down the centre and scoop away the pulpy seeds.

crème fraîche, fromage frais and mascarpone as creams of every description are the no-cook's best friend, turning into instant silky sauces. Go for light crème fraîche and zero-fat fromage frais, if you wish. Mascarpone is the most de luxe of all – beat it until just soft if it's too stiff.

cooked and smoked meats because they're convenient and usually very tasty. Try different cooked chickens – BBQ, Oriental, chargrilled – plus smoked chicken, turkey, duck and venison, as well as hams – even crisp-fried bacon bits.

breads as the right bread establishes an instant atmosphere. Serve Italian breads with Mediterranean foods, pittas with Middle Eastern, rye with seafood and Scandinavian flavours, and turn wraps and tortillas into new-wave sandwiches.

rocket, watercress and mustard and cress because they add a peppery bite. Use mustard and cress for sprinkling. Choose mixed bags of salad with care – they can contain too many types of leaf.

unsalted butter as salted butter may be fine for cooking and everyday use, but unsalted tastes cleaner and more refined, and can be used for sweet dishes as well as savoury.

custard because you can use it to whip up a quick dessert, and as a base for homemade ice cream and other glitzy desserts.

## in the freezer

frozen peas and broad beans as they add a fresh, sweet note. Put in a bowl with a little salt, cover with boiling water and leave for 10 minutes. Drain, cool quickly in cold water and drain again.

ice cream because a tub of best-quality vanilla ice cream can be transformed in no time into a memorable dessert by stirring through extra ingredients such as chopped chocolate, nuts, marshmallows... you name it.

wraps, breads and muffins as they defrost in minutes for exciting hand-held lunches and suppers. Breads can be sliced from frozen and toasted into bruschettas and crostini, muffins crumbled for instant trifles.

prawns because they can be used to make a quick feast.

## 5 great no-cook spices

crushed chillies Keep a small bowl on the table and you'll find you use them almost as much as black pepper. Good whenever you want a flavour lift.

cinnamon A warm brown spice that goes beautifully with apples, stone fruits and Moroccan dishes. Try grinding cinnamon sticks in your coffee grinder for a marvellously deep, rich flavour and aroma.

poppy seeds Add crunch and a faint aniseed flavour to dishes with this delicate and pretty spice. Caraway seeds give a similar whiff of the exotic.

paprika Use paprika to dust over egg and vegetable dishes to give an appetizing appearance and a gently spiced first bite.

smoked paprika One of the boldest and most exciting flavours in the entire spice-box. Use infrequently, in careful quantities, to give panache to chargrilled and spicy dishes.

On page 158 you'll also find a list of things I recommend you have in your storecupboard to make no-cooking easier.

we live in an age of ready meals and
takeaways – although these continue to get better and
better, for a little extra effort you can make far more creative
and exciting meals without the bother of cooking

# instant suppers
## and lunches

# crunchy duck and noodles

**Serves 4 ● 15–20 minutes to prepare, keeps its crunch for 24 hours**

**Conjure this up when you fancy something light but tasty – it's also good for a lunchbox. The best bit of the crunch comes from the water chestnuts, which squeak as you bite.**

What you need
450g/1lb cooked duck, on the bone, or
    350g/12oz off (Chinese restaurants sell
    cooked and BBQ duck – you'll need half
    a duck)
150g/5oz fresh beansprouts
half 220g can of water chestnuts, drained,
    rinsed and thinly sliced
2 spring onions, shredded
1cm/½inch cube of fresh ginger, peeled and
    finely chopped
handful of fresh coriander, chopped

Make sure you've got
instant Chinese noodles (150g/5oz)
boiling water
1 red chilli
hoisin sauce (2 tbsp)
dry sherry (2 tbsp)
toasted sesame oil (2 tsp)
dark soy sauce (2 tbsp)
an orange

❶ Break up the noodles into a pan or bowl and pour a kettleful of boiling water over them to cover generously. Leave for 5–10 minutes.
❷ Meanwhile, discard the skin and bones from the duck and shred the rest (do this with your hands). Try and keep it in long thin pieces.
❸ Mix the duck, beansprouts, chestnuts, spring onions, ginger and half a chilli, deseeded and finely chopped. Drain the noodles when ready and add these.
❹ Whisk the hoisin, sherry, sesame oil and soy sauce together and toss into the mixture (you probably won't need salt). Sprinkle over the coriander and orange juice.

**Drain the remaining water chestnuts, put in a bowl, cover with water and they'll then keep in the fridge for up to a week. Slice them thinly for salads and stir-fries.**

make it your own **You can use 3 celery stalks instead of the water chestnuts – slice them very thinly at an angle. ● You can also make this dish with cooked or barbecued chicken. Squeeze lemon juice over it instead of orange.**

# coconut turkey noodles

**Serves 4 ● 15-25 minutes to prepare**

**This makes a satisfying supper at relatively little cost, but is sufficiently intriguing in flavour to serve when entertaining guests.**

**What you need**

400g/14oz cooked turkey (or chicken or
  pork), preferably BBQ or chargrilled if you
  can get it, cut into bite-sized chunks
2 spring onions, shredded
1 yellow, orange or red pepper, deseeded and
  thinly sliced
6 cherry tomatoes, halved or quartered
150ml/¼pint coconut cream

**Make sure you've got**

instant Chinese noodles (150g/5oz)
boiling water
½ red chilli, finely chopped
tomato ketchup (2 tsp)
Worcestershire sauce

❶ Put the noodles in a bowl, cover with boiling water and leave for 5–10 minutes. Drain in a sieve or colander.
❷ While the noodles are soaking, put the turkey, spring onions, chilli, pepper and tomatoes in a bowl. Pour over the coconut cream, ketchup, a dash of Worcestershire sauce and some seasoning, and mix.
❸ Stir in the noodles to mix thoroughly, then divide between 4 plates.

make it your own To give this dish a Hawaiian feel, you can sprinkle it with 45g/1¹/₂oz chopped roasted macadamia nuts (which are indigenous to the islands) for a crunchy topping.

# tuna artichoke pitta breads (simple)

**Makes 3 large pittas ● 10-20 minutes to make**

**What you need**

3 large pittas, halved

100ml/3½fl oz full-fat or light crème fraîche

115g/4oz artichokes in oil, drained and sliced

2 large tomatoes, halved, deseeded and sliced

small bunch of mint, chopped

**Make sure you've got**

pesto (2 tsp)

canned tuna in oil (200g)

pine nuts (2 tbsp)

a lemon

❶  If you like, warm the pitta breads under the grill or in a toaster.

❷  Mix the crème fraîche and pesto in a medium bowl. Pile in the drained and flaked tuna, the artichokes, the flaked pine nuts, sliced tomatoes and mint, and mix lightly.

❸  Spoon the filling into the pittas and squeeze over some lemon juice.

# smoked turkey and mango wraps

**Serves 4 (easily halved or quartered) ● 10-20 minutes to prepare**

**What you need**

4 soft wheat tortillas or wraps, about 20cm/8in

200g/7oz sliced smoked turkey or chicken

10cm/4inch piece of cucumber, peeled, halved
   lengthwise and sliced

2 handfuls of watercress, roughly chopped

1 ripe mango, peeled and cut into thick sticks

a few basil leaves

**Make sure you've got**

mayonnaise (125ml/4fl oz)

curry paste (2 tsp – check the small print on
   your curry paste as some brands need
   cooking; if so, dry-fry the paste for a
   couple of minutes, or sizzle in the
   microwave)

❶ Mix the mayo and curry paste. Keeping 2.5cm/1in from the edge, spread a tortilla with a quarter of the mayo.

❷ Add a quarter each of the turkey, cucumber, watercress, mango and basil.

❸ If the wraps are to go, get ready a square of cling film. Tuck in the sides of the wrap, then roll firmly to enfold the filling completely. Slice at an angle down the centre and secure with the cling film. Continue with the rest of the wraps.

# tuna in the Tunisian style

**Serves 4 ● 10-20 minutes to prepare**

**Almost everything needed to make this dish can be found in the well-stocked no-cook storecupboard.**

**What you need**

400g can of tuna in oil, drained

400g can of chickpeas, drained 2 miniature
pickled lemons, such as Belazu,
    thinly sliced and seeds discarded

bunch of mint, chopped

1 lettuce, preferably Cos or romaine

**Make sure you've got**

16–24 stoned green or red olives, halved

8 strips of sun-dried tomato in oil, drained

1 garlic clove

ground coriander (1 tsp)

caraway seeds (1 tsp, optional)

harissa paste (1 tsp)

olive oil (2 tbsp)

red wine vinegar (2 tbsp)

1 lemon, quartered

❶ Mix together the tuna, chickpeas, olives, pickled lemons and mint.

❷ Make the dressing: in a blender or processor, whiz together the sun-dried tomatoes, garlic, coriander, caraway if using, harissa, olive oil and vinegar – the dressing should be quite thick and sticky.

❸ Stir the dressing into the chickpeas.

❹ Arrange the lettuce leaves on 4 plates – in a starfish formation if you are feeling creative – heap on the chickpeas and serve with lemon quarters to squeeze over.

You can complete the salad up to a day ahead – the flavour even improves.

make it your own Serve with couscous: measure out 400 ml / 14 fl oz of boiling water in a jug and add $1\frac{1}{2}$ tsp good-quality bouillon powder (preferably Marigold), 1 tbsp olive oil and 225g / 8 oz couscous. Leave for 10 minutes, stirring occasionally.

# pan bagna *(simple)*

**Serves 4 (easily halved or doubled)** ● **15-20 minutes to prepare**

**This dish from Nice is a sort of salade niçoise sandwich. It is best made 2 to 24 hours ahead, and travels brilliantly wrapped in foil.**

**What you need**

a loaf of country-style bread, preferably a thin
    round one about 20 cm/8 in in diameter
5 small juicy tomatoes, sliced
large handful of basil (at least 20 leaves)
small handful of mint (at least 10 leaves)
160g jar of white tuna in water, or best-quality
    canned tuna, drained
1 shallot or 2 spring onions, shredded

**Make sure you've got**

1 garlic clove, cut in half
extra-virgin olive oil (3 tbsp)
red wine vinegar (2 tsp)
capers (3 tsp), drained and rinsed
12 black olives, halved
8 anchovy fillets, preferably white
    anchovies in oil, drained and sliced

❶ Slice the loaf across its depth to make 2 thin discs. Scrape out as much of the fluffy white bread in the middle as you can, to make space for the filling.
❷ Rub the inside of each piece with garlic, to impart a subtle hint of the Riviera.
❸ Drizzle half the oil over one cut side of the bread, followed by half the vinegar. Scatter in half the tomatoes, season well, then top with half the herbs. Pile in the tuna, spreading it all over, then scatter the shallot or spring onions, capers, olives and anchovies evenly. Add the remaining herbs and tomatoes. Drizzle the other piece of bread with the remaining oil and vinegar, and use as a lid for the sandwich.
❹ Squeeze together, wrap tightly in foil and leave at room temperature for a couple of hours, or in the fridge overnight, but bring back to room temperature to eat.

You can make individual pan bagnas in rolls. Spread the filling right over the sandwich area so you don't end up with a barren patch round the perimeter.

## make it your own You can customize this in many different ways, though the use of good bread, the best tuna you can buy (look out for jars), salted capers (rather than pickled), good olives and anchovies will immediately take it into the first division. ● Good additions or substitutions are chargrilled peppers, sunblushed tomatoes, fresh tarragon and flavoured oils.

# lemony chicken couscous

**Serves 4 (easily halved) ● 20-30 minutes to prepare**

**What you need**

250g/9oz couscous

2 spring onions, shredded

2 large tomatoes, cored, deseeded and roughly
    chopped

400g/14oz cooked chargrilled chicken, cut into
    bite-sized pieces

2 miniature preserved lemons (such as
    Belazu), seeds and flesh discarded, finely
    sliced ($^{1}/_{4}$ of a large preserved lemon)

**Make sure you've got**

finely grated zest of $^{1}/_{2}$ lemon

good-quality bouillon powder, preferably
    Marigold ($1^{1}/_{2}$ tsp)

olive oil (1 tbsp)

boiling water (400ml/14fl oz)

harissa paste (1-2 tsp)

❶ Make the couscous by stirring the couscous, lemon zest and bouillon powder together and pouring over the olive oil and boiling water. Cover loosely with cling film and leave to stand for 10 minutes, fluffing up occasionally with a fork.

❷ Meanwhile, make the lemon chicken by mixing the spring onions, tomatoes and harissa till blended. Stir in the chicken and the preserved lemons.

❸ Arrange the couscous and the chicken side by side on plates.

# hoisin chicken, plums and noodles

**Serves 4 (easily doubled or halved) ● 15-25 minutes to prepare**

**Almost everything needed to make this dish can be found in the well-stocked no-cook storecupboard.**

**What you need**
Two 190g packs of Chinese-flavoured or
    maple-roast cooked chicken
250g pack of beansprouts
5 mi-cuit plums (see below), or soaked
    prunes

**Make sure you've got**
1 red chilli, deseeded and thinly sliced
instant rice noodles (about 125g/4oz)
boiling water, to cover
rice wine vinegar (2 tsp)
soy sauce (1 tsp)
hoisin sauce (2 tbsp)
fresh ginger (1 cm/$\frac{1}{2}$inch ), grated
sunflower or other vegetable oil (4 tbsp)

❶ Slice the chicken and put it in a bowl. Mix with the beansprouts and chilli. Slice the plums or prunes.

❷ Snap the noodles in half or into 3 and put in a bowl. Cover with boiling water and leave for 4 minutes, or as directed on the packet. Drain and mix into the chicken mixture.

❸ Meanwhile, mix the vinegar, soy sauce, hoisin sauce, ginger and oil together, and stir into the chicken and noodles. Serve at once.

If you wash root ginger, there is no need to go through the fiddly process of peeling it – the skin is perfectly edible.

Mi-cuit plums are luscious plump semi-dried prunes. If you can't find them, you will need the moistest prunes you can find or, better still, ones that have been covered in boiling water and left to soak overnight.

# tomato mozzarella piémontaise

**Serves 4 ● 10-20 minutes to prepare**

**This cross between a tomato and mozzarella salad and peppers piémontaise, in which peppers are stuffed with tomatoes and anchovies and baked, makes a great supper, but is also good as part of a buffet.**

**What you need**

4 juicy tomatoes, halved through their equators
    and the seeds and pulp removed
50g/2oz chargrilled peppers, sliced
125g/4oz buffalo mozzarella, cubed
handful of basil leaves

**Make sure you've got**

2 anchovies, rinsed, drained and chopped
extra-virgin olive oil (1 tbsp)
4 fat brown olives, stoned and halved

## ahead

❶ Lay the tomato halves on a plate and season lightly.
❷ Mix the peppers, mozzarella and anchovies in a bowl. Pour over the oil, mix lightly and spoon into the tomato halves – they should be full to overflowing. If convenient, you can leave the dish for up to 4 hours at this point.

## at the last minute

❸ Casually scatter the basil leaves over the tomatoes. Top each with half an olive and eat. If the sun isn't shining, imagine it is.

## make it your own
Spanish piquillo peppers are great for this dish. ● If you have a lemon- or basil-scented extra-virgin olive oil, this is the time to use it.

# Thai beef and cucumber

**Serves 4 (easily doubled) ● 10-20 minutes to prepare**

**This is an example of fusion food, where New York (pastrami) meets Bangkok (everything else). If you want to make this dish look effortless, you can measure everything, cut the pastrami and slice the vegetables an hour or two ahead – but don't assemble until just before serving.**

**What you need**
125g/4oz pastrami (from the deli)
1 cucumber (about 450g/1lb) peeled, halved,
    seeds scooped out with a spoon and thinly
    sliced
1 shallot, very thinly sliced
150g bag of crisp lettuce leaves
handful of coriander and of mint, roughly
    chopped

**Make sure you've got**
1 small red chilli, very thinly sliced
clear honey (1 tbsp)
Japanese rice wine or dry sherry (3 tbsp)
good pinch of red pepper (chilli) flakes

## ahead
❶ Slice the pastrami at an angle into strips. Mix with the cucumber, shallot and sliced chilli, using your fingers to separate the thin slices of pastrami.

## at the last minute
❷ Whisk the honey, rice wine or sherry and chilli flakes together, and fold into the meat mixture.
❸ Arrange the lettuce on a platter. Spoon the meat mixture over the centre, drizzling any dressing left in the bowl over the lettuce. Serve covered with a blanket of coriander and mint.

# toasting success

When it comes to bread-based snacks, the Italians know every trick in the book. Bruschetta is a Tuscan invention – originally used to test the quality of the new-season's olive oil. Thick slices of Italian bread – authentically country bread such as pugliese – are toasted on both sides in a toaster or under a grill, then rubbed with a cut garlic clove, drizzled with extra-virgin olive oil and sprinkled with coarse salt. The toast should be crisp on the outside and soft in the centre, and ideally enjoyed hot from the grill. Toppings are not strictly necessary, but, if you are offering them, choose bread with a strong crust, or plan to eat them with a knife and fork. Toppings should have strong flavours and contrasting colours – let everyone help themselves.

**1** use your best oil This is an occasion when speciality oils – extra-virgin, or oil infused with lemon or basil – will come into their own (after all, bruschetta was invented to showcase their flavours). Don't mask the taste of these extra-fine oils with toppings, but don't forget to rub the bread with garlic and sprinkle on some coarse salt.

**2** Catalan bruschettas Although this bruschetta variation is practised all over Italy, I first came across it in Spain. The idea is to give the bruschetta a final rub with the cut side of a super-ripe, juicy tomato. Season and serve as is, or as a base for other toppings.

**3** tapenade bruschettas Spread the bruschettas with tapenade or olive paste and top with wedges of plum tomato or thick slices of cucumber cut at an angle.

**4** smoked Cheddar, tomato and basil bruschettas Put a thin slice of smoked Cheddar on a bruschetta, top with a slice of tomato or strip of sun-dried tomato and a basil leaf.

**5** pesto and mozzarella bruschetta Spread bruschetta with pesto – classic basil, olive or red pepper – and top with a slice of fresh mozzarella cheese.

**6** Parma ham and fig bruschettas Spread bruschettas with Dolcelatte cheese and top with a curl of Parma ham (or another thinly sliced smoked meat, such as turkey) and a quarter of a fresh fig. A leaf of purple basil is a pretty finishing touch.

**7** pâté and pepper bruschettas Spread bruschettas with a coarse pâté and top with a slice of chargrilled pepper from a jar of antipasto – or a slice of piquillo pepper.

**8** crostini Crostini are usually made from finely textured ciabatta bread, or slices of French baguette. More petite than bruschetta, they can be untoasted or toasted, and are usually served cold as a starter or canapé, spread with something tasty rather than acting as a base for things piled on top. Sometimes they are toasted until completely crisp and then rubbed with garlic and drizzled with oil like bruschetta – and this is how I like them. You can sometimes buy packs of ready-made crostini in bakery sections, but they are pretty dull compared to the real thing.

**9** creamy Gorgonzola crostini Mix Gorgonzola with an equal quantity of mascarpone. Spread on the crostini and top with a teaspoon of tapenade or chopped olives, and snipped chives.

**10** pizza-flavoured crostini Lay a chopped anchovy on a crostini and mash in. Top with slices of juicy tomato and a sliver of Parmesan.

Parma ham and fig bruschetta

pizza-flavoured crostini

creamy Gorgonzola crostini

pâté and pepper bruschetta

# glamorous
## nibbles
### and starters

no need to spend ages making elaborate
canapés and first courses, just assemble
clever combinations of food and
present them beautifully – the
spirit of no-cooking

# smoked haddock carpaccio

**Serves 4 ● 10 minutes to prepare (but start a good hour ahead)**

**Here smoked haddock is very thinly sliced to look delicate and elegant, resembling smoked salmon.**

**What you need**
200g/7oz piece of undyed smoked haddock
    fillet, preferably the thick part of the fillet

**Make sure you've got**
capers (1tbsp), chopped
extra-virgin olive oil (1tbsp)
$\frac{1}{2}$ lemon

**for the dressing**
2 spring onions, shredded
small handful of parsley, finely chopped

## ahead
❶ Put the haddock in the freezer for 15-20 minutes to make it easier to slice.
❷ Sharpen your knife. Trim off the edges of the fillet so you are left with only the fleshy central section; discard the edges (you may have as much as 50g/2oz of waste, but don't worry, it's worth it).
❸ Now slice down into the fillet, against the grain, to make long, very thin rectangles of fish fillet. You should get 30-40 very thin slices from the fillet. Lay these on a large plate to cover it completely. Try to scrape the slices from the skin as you go, or trim the skin off each slice, discarding the skin.

## at the last minute
❹ About 20 minutes before serving, scatter with the dressing ingredients one by one, finishing with plenty of black pepper.
❺ Serve accompanied by bread and butter.

This dish can only be made with undyed smoked haddock, which is a pale creamy colour. The bright yellow dyed type is to be avoided.

## make it your own Doyenne of British food Henrietta Green, who taught me this recipe, tells me you can treat cold roast beef (preferably rare), chicken and turkey in exactly the same way.

# potted prawns marinara

**Serves 6 (easily halved or multiplied) ● 10-20 minutes to prepare (needs 2 hours to chill)**

**This is a variation on that old-fashioned British classic, potted shrimps.**

**What you need**

250g/9oz king prawns, or other prawns,
  defrosted and drained if frozen

1 tbsp red pepper or other red pesto

**Make sure you've got**

butter (125g/4oz)

1 anchovy fillet, rinsed (optional)

tomato purée or sun-dried tomato purée (1tbsp)

Worcestershire sauce

Tabasco sauce

bread for toast, to serve

## ahead

❶ Melt the butter.

❷ Roughly chop the prawns, finely chop the anchovy and mix with the tomato purée, pesto, a splash each of Worcestershire and Tabasco sauce, and some seasoning. Mix in the butter.

❸ If you are planning to turn out the potted prawns, line the bases of 6 small (100ml/3$^1$/$_2$ fl oz) ramekins with little discs of baking paper. If planning to serve them in the ramekins, there is no need to do this. Pack in the prawn mixture and chill for a couple of hours until set, or up to 24 hours.

## at the last minute

❹ Either serve the prawns as they are or run a knife round the edge and turn them out. If they don't come out easily, dip the bases briefly in boiling water and try again.

**Serve with lots of freshly made toast on which to spread the prawns.**

# prawn and melon cocktail

**Serves 4 ● 15-30 minutes to prepare, depending on your melon-balling skills**

**If you plan to serve this for larger numbers it is a bit arduous making the melon balls, unless you can buy them ready-prepared.**

**What you need**
200g/7oz shelled prawns, defrosted if
   necessary, drained and dried
675g/1$^1$/$_2$ lb green or orange melon flesh, cut
   into small cubes or balls (or 250g ready-
   prepared melon balls)
crisp lettuce leaves

**Make sure you've got**
chilli flakes ($^1$/$_4$ tsp)
mayonnaise (125ml/4fl oz)
smoked paprika, for dusting

## ahead
❶ Mix the prawns and melon, and leave to drain in a small sieve set over a bowl. You can do this a day ahead.

## at the last minute
❷ Discard the liquid that has collected in the bowl. Mix the chilli into the mayonnaise, then fold into the prawns and melon.
❸ Arrange the lettuce on plates and season lightly. Arrange the cocktail on top, dust with smoked paprika and serve.

## make it your own If you use 2 small melons, you can serve the cocktail in their
hollowed-out shells rather than on lettuce leaves. Leave the melon halves to drain upside down.
● For the slightly more adventurous, whisk 1 tsp of curry paste into the mayonnaise. (See the note about curry paste on page 14.)

smoked salmon savvy

One of the most wonderful of no-cook treats, smoked salmon is glamorous, tasty and versatile. It is thin and delicate enough to be used as a wrapping for other foods and makes an attractive focal point in its own right. Smoked salmon varies hugely in quality: the best is translucent, firm and with widely spaced markings. Unless you wish to impress with your knife skills, always buy it pre-sliced. Trimmings are cheaper, and useful in many dishes.

1 lunch to go Spread a wrap with 1 tablespoon of mayo and lay over that some smoked salmon, lots of mustard and cress and sliced tomato. Squeeze over some lemon juice, grind over some pepper, tuck in the sides and roll up. Cut in half and eat.

2 fabulous finger food Whip a 142ml carton of double cream or 150ml/¼ pint of crème fraîche until just beginning to thicken, and add 1 tablespoon of grated horseradish or horseradish sauce and 1 tablespoon of lemon juice. Roughly cut up 125g/4oz peeled cooked king prawns and fold in. Season. Lay out the salmon slices one by one (you will need 250g/9oz), top with a dollop of the cream mixture at the narrow end and roll up to make short thick rolls. Dust the ends with paprika before serving – enough for 6 as a canapé/starter.

3 glitzy canapé Cut 200g/7oz smoked salmon into 9cm/3½in squares. Put in the centre of each a teaspoon of Boursin (either the pepper or garlic-and-fine-herb type). Gather at the top and tie with a chive. For 8 bite-sized purses you will need one 80g Boursin cheese plus 8 stout chives.

4 glamorous garnish Take a 450g/1lb salmon fillet. Cut 50g/2oz of smoked salmon into thin strips and arrange as a lattice on the fish, tucking the ends underneath. Serve with a simple sauce of chopped fresh dill stirred into crème fraîche.

5 goats' cheese bites Take a 100g/3½oz log of goats' cheese and wrap it in cling film. Roll it out until 3cm/1¼in diameter and about 18cm/7in long, wrap in smoked salmon (you'll need about 85g/3oz) and chill for at least an hour or overnight. Sharpen your knife and slice it into10–12 bites.

**6** stylish poppadums Pile a teaspoon of bought tzatziki (or make your own from 5cm/2in cucumber, trimmed and sliced, some chopped mint, a scrap of garlic and 142ml carton of Greek yoghurt) into the centre of mini-poppadums. Top a third with a twist of smoked salmon, a third with a peeled cooked king prawn and a third with a spoonful of Avruga (herring) caviar. (For 20 mini-poppadums, you will need 75g/3oz tzatziki, 50g/2oz smoked salmon, about 35g/1¼oz king prawns, 7–8 teaspoons of Avruga.). Do this at the last minute or they go soft.

**7** toasted treat Spread toasted pikelets or crumpets with mascarpone, then top with smoked salmon – and Avruga (herring) caviar, if you have some. For 4 crumpets you will need about 75g/3oz mascarpone and the same of smoked salmon. Great for brunch.

**8** crunchy with cocktails Finely chop 50g/2oz smoked salmon (or smoked salmon pieces) with a little coriander and ground black pepper. Divide 2 or 3 heads of chicory into leaves and put a teaspoon into each leaf.

**9** posh starter Line 6 small ramekins or coffee cups with cling film, then line with smoked salmon, slicing into strips as necessary and leaving enough over-hanging to fold over the top (you will need about 200–300g/7–10½oz). Put 275g/10oz smoked trout fillets in a processor with 1 tablespoon of chopped fresh dill, one 150g tub of cottage cheese, one 142ml/¼pint tub of sour cream and the juice of ½ lemon. Season well with pepper (it probably won't need any more salt), then spoon into the ramekins and fold over the smoked salmon. Chill overnight, then turn out, peel off the cling film and serve as a first course for 6.

**10** salad in a flash Toss strips of smoked salmon and king prawns into a lettuce, cucumber and tomato salad. Grate over a little lemon zest, dress with lemon vinaigrette and scatter with basil leaves or snipped chives to serve.

toasted treats

crunchy with cocktails

salad in a flash

posh starter

# fruity anchoïade

**Serves 4 as a spread or dip ● 5-10 minutes to prepare**

**What you need**
4 plump ready-to-eat dried figs
1 fresh red pepper, roughly chopped
good handful of fresh parsley

**Make sure you've got**
extra-virgin olive oil (2tbsp)
6 anchovies, rinsed and squeezed dry
squeeze of lemon juice

❶ Mix everything together and whiz in the processor.
❷ Serve with bread or crudités. Ask guests to guess what's in the dip.

Salted anchovies, which you can buy in tins and jars, have a more pungent taste and I prefer them for this recipe.

## make it your own In true Middle Eastern style, you can add all sorts of exotica to the basic recipe – rosewater, a scrap of preserved lemon, a flick of orange zest – to heighten the mystery.

# green anchoïade

**Serves 4 as a spread or dip ● 5-10 minutes to prepare**

**What you need**
handful of mixed fresh herbs, including
    parsley, mint and basil
1 tbsp pine nuts

**Make sure you've got**
1 large garlic clove
2 anchovies, drained
1 lemon
extra-virgin olive oil (175ml/6fl oz)
capers (1 tbsp), drained, rinsed and chopped
    (optional)

❶ In a food processor, whiz the garlic until finely chopped, then add the herbs and anchovies.
❷ With the machine still running, add the juice from the lemon and the oil with some seasoning (add salt with care because of the anchovies) to form a beautiful green emulsion.
❸ Stir in the capers, if you like them, and the pine nuts.

# rum tapenade

**Serves 4 or more as part of a dip selection ● 10-15 minutes to prepare**

**What you need**
2 spring onions
1tbsp dark rum

**Make sure you've got**
anchovies (25g/1oz), rinsed
1 garlic clove
good pinch of crushed chillies
black olives (125g/4oz), stoned
extra-virgin (2tbsp) olive oil
squeeze of lemon juice

❶ In a food processor, whiz the spring onions, anchovies, garlic and chillies until mashed.
❷ Add the olives and whiz again until these are coarsely chopped.
❸ With the motor still running, add the oil, lemon juice and rum.
❹ Serve with toasted pitta breads.

# cannellini bean hummus

**Serves 6 or more as part of a dip selection ● 10-15 minutes to prepare**

**What you need**
1 spring onion
400g can of cannellini beans, rinsed and drained
2 tbsp tahini or light tahini (or even peanut butter)
pitta breads, to serve

**Make sure you've got**
1 garlic clove
olive oil (2 tbsp, plus more for drizzling)
1 slice (25g/1oz) of white bread, soaked in
    water and immediately squeezed out
zest of $\frac{1}{2}$ lemon
ground coriander ($\frac{1}{2}$ tsp)
ground cumin (1 tsp, plus more for dusting)

❶ In a food processor, whiz the spring onion and garlic until finely chopped.
❷ Add the beans and process to a dry purée, then add the tahini, oil, bread, lemon zest and spices.
❸ With the motor still running, add 3-4 tbsp cold water to lighten the texture of the dip.
❹ Spread thinly over a medium-sized plate. Drizzle over some oil and dust with cumin. Serve with pitta breads.

fruity anchoïade

rum tapenade

cannellini bean hummus

green anchoïade

# smoked duck with papaya

**Serves 4 as a dainty fusion-style starter ● 10-20 minutes to prepare**

**What you need**

1 ripe papaya

1 smoked duck breast, about 225g/8oz

**for the sauce**

150ml/¼ pint coconut cream (from a carton)

1tsp creamed coconut (from a block, optional)

finely grated zest of ¼ lime

½ tsp tamarind paste (from a jar, optional)

12 basil leaves

**Make sure you've got**

soy sauce

Tabasco sauce

Worcestershire sauce

## ahead

❶ Peel the papaya with a small knife and halve it. Discard the caviar-like seeds and slice the flesh neatly. Put on a plate, cover with cling film and chill until ready to eat.

❷ Slice the fat off the duck breast and discard. Cut the flesh into thin neat slices. Cover with cling film and chill.

❸ Whisk the coconut cream and creamed coconut together until creamy, and add the lime zest, tamarind, a splash each of soy sauce, Tabasco and Worcestershire sauce and the basil leaves, torn if large. Chill until ready to serve.

## at the last minute

❹ Pour the sauce over 4 smallish plates (this is called 'flooding' the plates). Arrange the duck and papaya in alternate slices on the sauce and serve.

**Papaya is a good-natured fruit, in that it will remain ripe without going over for up to 4 days.**

# classic celeriac rémoulade with Parma ham

**Serves 4 (easily doubled, but cutting the celeriac is a bit of bore for larger numbers) ● 20-30 minutes to prepare**

**What you need**
450g / 1 lb fresh celeriac
100g pack of prosciutto di Parma (Parma ham)

**Make sure you've got**
½ lemon
boiling water, to cover
mayonnaise (125 ml / 4 fl oz, bought or homemade, see page 87)
mustard (2 tsp, preferably wholegrain)
capers (1 tsp), rinsed
2 cornichons (gherkins), rinsed and chopped
good bunch of parsley or tarragon, chopped

## ahead
❶ Squeeze the lemon half into a large heatproof bowl. Peel the celeriac, removing all the brown bits. Slice it thinly, then slice these again into matchsticks, putting them into the bowl and tossing in the lemon as you go. Take a tip from professional food stylists and discard any mis-shapes or stubs – although thriftiness is to be applauded, they will make the finished dish look scruffy.
❷ Cover with boiling water, put a lid or plate over the bowl and leave for 5 minutes. Drain and refresh in cold water, then drain again and dry on kitchen paper.
❸ Make the dressing by mixing together the mayonnaise, mustard, capers, cornichons and parsley or tarragon. Toss the celeriac in the dressing, ensuring all is well covered. You can leave it for up to 4 hours at this point.

## at the last minute
❹ Cut the ham into bite-sized strips and arrange these, ribbon style, round the edge of the plate. Heap the salad in the centre. Grind over some pepper and serve.

# watermelon, feta and nut salad (simple)

**Serves 4 as a side dish or first course (easily halved or multiplied for large gatherings) ● 10-15 minutes to prepare (presentation is important)**

**Middle Eastern in origin, this is one of the prettiest salads I know. It looks best in a large glass bowl or individual glass dishes.**

**What you need**
500g/1 lb 2oz slice of fresh watermelon
    (425g/15oz prepared weight)
150g/5oz feta cheese
25g/1oz toasted chopped hazelnuts

**Make sure you've got**
olive oil (2 tbsp)
squeeze of lemon juice

❶ Dice the watermelon flesh into neat 2cm/$^3$/$_4$inch cubes. Cut the feta into slightly smaller cubes.

❷ Toss these together in a bowl, adding the nuts, oil and plenty of black pepper.

❸ If you make this more than a few minutes ahead, the watermelon will give off quite a lot of water, so at the last minute transfer the salad to your serving bowl with a slotted spoon. Squeeze over some lemon juice and serve.

**The quality of the feta is important: some of the prepacked types can be dry and salty. Far better to buy it loose in oil from the cheese counter.**

## make it your own **If you do buy feta in oil, use the oil in the dressing. Alternatively use lemon-infused olive oil. ● Use sliced pistachios or pumpkin seeds instead of the hazelnuts.**

**LEFT** classic celeriac rémoulade with Parma ham **ABOVE** watermelon, feta and nut salad

# fresh cream of avocado soup

**Serves 6 (easily halved) ● 15-25 minutes to prepare, plus chilling and an extra 5 minutes if making the salsa**

**A ravishing pale green in colour, this is the prettiest soup I know. You can see why they went for bathroom suites this shade in the 1970s. It may seem anathema to add water to something that is already very subtle in flavour, but it emulsifies with the avocado to give a divine texture. The soup is very rich, so serve it in small bowls.**

| What you need | Make sure you've got |
|---|---|
| 2 spring onions | 2 garlic cloves |
| 4 fresh avocados | $1/2$ lemon |
| 6 mint leaves | Tabasco sauce |
| 284 ml carton of single cream | Worcestershire sauce |
| snipped chives or salsa (see below) | |

❶ Blitz the spring onions and garlic in the processor until smashed.

❷ Add the avocado flesh, mint, a squeeze of lemon juice, a splash each of Tabasco and Worcestershire sauce, and plenty of seasoning.

❸ Pour in the cream and whiz, then pulse in 300 ml/$1/2$ pint water, which will give the texture an almost ethereal lightness. The soup should be as thick as semi-whipped cream; add a little extra water if necessary.

❹ Chill well for an hour. If leaving longer, squeeze a little extra lemon juice over the surface to keep it a fresh jade green.

❺ Serve very cold, with snipped chives or a blob of salsa.

**Make a quick salsa by roughly processing a spring onion with $1/2$ red chilli, $1/2$ red pepper and a medium-sized tomato, making sure you keep some texture. Season well and divide between the 6 bowls. This makes about 150 ml/$1/4$ pint.**

## make it your own **You can give this more of a Mexican theme by serving it with corn tortilla chips.**

# cucumber and watercress vichyssoise

**Serves 4 ● 10-15 minutes to prepare, but chilling**

**Seasoned well and served very cold, this makes a rich and creamy start to a meal.**

**What you need**

5 spring onions, including about 5 cm / 2 in of
    green top, roughly cut up

3 - 4 sprigs of mint

85g bag of watercress

1 cucumber (about 450g/1 lb), peeled (takes
    a second with a potato peeler), halved and
    the seeds scooped out

142 ml carton of single cream

chives, to decorate

**Make sure you've got**

$1/2$ garlic clove

$1/2$ lemon

dry sherry (2tbsp)

nutmeg

❶ In your food processor, blitz the garlic as finely as possible, then add the spring onion and mint. Wipe down the sides with a spatula, then add the watercress, followed by the cucumber, cut into chunks. Process until it forms a wet paste.

❷ Add the cream. Season well with salt, pepper, juice from the lemon half, sherry and freshly grated nutmeg.

❸ Chill for at least an hour and up to 24 hours. Serve in small bowls with snipped chives.

Chilled or frozen mixtures require much more seasoning or sweetening than those served at room temperature or hot. (If you have tasted melted ice cream, you will know how sweet it seems.) In this case, check the soup is well seasoned before it goes into the fridge and again before serving.

# sun-blushed gazpacho

**Serves 4 (easily multiplied – you can serve mini-portions in coffee cups or shot glasses as an appetizer)**

● **10-20 minutes to prepare**

**This makes an amazingly beautiful, sunset-coloured soup.**

**What you need**

25g/1oz sun-blushed or sun-dried tomatoes

350g/12oz good ripe tomatoes

2 spring onions

about 10cm/4in length of cucumber

**To garnish**

chopped green pepper

chopped cucumber

strips of sun-blushed tomato

strips of chargrilled red pepper

stoned green and black olives

**Make sure you've got**

crustless good white bread (125g/4oz)

1 garlic clove

$\frac{1}{2}$ small red chilli

sherry or red wine vinegar (2tbsp)

extra-virgin olive oil (2tbsp)

❶ Put the bread in a bowl of water and then squeeze it out gently. Put it in the food processor.

❷ Chop the sun-blushed or sun-dried tomatoes into the processor, then add the fresh tomatoes, spring onions and garlic. Peel the cucumber, halve it down the centre and scrape out the seeds. Roughly chop and add to processor along with chilli, vinegar and oil. Whiz for a couple of minutes until really smooth, scraping down the sides a couple of times. Taste and adjust the seasoning, then chill for at least half an hour. You can make this a day ahead if convenient.

❸ To serve, check the seasoning again, as being as cold as this tends to dim flavours. You can thin the soup, if you wish, with iced water, but I like it quite thick. Some cooks strain it, but I again I prefer it *au naturel*. Serve with the garnishes.

make it your own The garnishes are an important feature of gazpacho, and you can lay them all out on a platter for guests to help themselves. The only proviso is that they should be cut small enough to be eaten with a soup spoon.

# Double Gloucester balls (simple)

**Makes 20 cocktail-sized balls ● 15-20 minutes to prepare (make the mixture ahead)**

**These ingenious little mouthfuls make perfect snacks with drinks.**

**What you need**
125g/4oz ricotta
125g/4oz grated Double Gloucester cheese
45g/1½oz chopped toasted hazelnuts

**Make sure you've got**
Tabasco sauce
Worcestershire sauce

## ahead

❶ In a bowl, mix the cheeses with a splash each of Tabasco and Worcestershire sauce and chill in the fridge. If you are in a hurry, spread the mixture out thinly – it will chill faster.

## at the last minute

❷ Put the nuts in a bowl. Take a teaspoon of the mixture and roll into a small ball. It is tempting to make them big, specially if you are impatient by nature, but they are much nicer small, no bigger than marbles.
❸ Drop the balls into the nuts, roll them around until they are well coated and put them on a serving plate. Continue till the mixture is used up.

## make it your own
**You can use another hard cheese instead of the Double Gloucester; smoked Cheddar packs a punch. ● You can use walnuts instead or hazelnuts, but they need to be very finely chopped. ● If you want to make tricolour balls, you can coat one-third of the balls with nuts, one-third with finely chopped herbs and one-third with paprika. You will, however, find that the nutty ones get scoffed first.**

# chilled Parmesan and chive soufflé

**Serves 6 ● 10-20 minutes to prepare (plus a 10-minute wait for the gelatine; make it at least 2 – and up to 24 – hours ahead)**

**This is a rather elegant and understated dish. Don't turn the page when you see the word gelatine – this really isn't difficult to do, and it's worth the trouble.**

**What you need**
2 tsp powdered gelatine (about ²/₃ of a sachet)
50g/2oz Parmesan cheese
handful of chives
284ml carton of double cream

**Make sure you've got**
good-quality bouillon powder, preferably
    Marigold (1tsp)
boiling water (150ml/¼pint)
2 eggs
cayenne pepper
paprika, for dusting
bread for toast, to serve

## ahead

❶ Mix the gelatine and bouillon in a bowl. Pour over the boiling water and whisk well until the gelatine is dissolved and smooth. Leave to cool to room temperature.
❷ Meanwhile, grate the cheese and snip the chives. Separate the eggs and beat the egg whites in a large bowl with a pinch of salt until they form soft peaks which fall when you remove the beaters. (Use the yolks for mayonnaise, page 87.)
❸ In another bowl, whip the cream till just stiff, not firm. Fold the cream into the egg whites, together with the cheese, chives and a pinch of cayenne.
❹ Pour into a 1litre/1³/₄ pint soufflé dish and leave to set.

## at the last minute

❺ Dust with paprika and serve with hot toast.

## make it your own Vary the herbs – finely chopped chervil or tarragon go well.

# memorable
# main courses

nowadays you can readily buy excellent precooked
chicken, turkey, duck and even seafood.
Think exciting main-course salads, captivating cold
collations and even the no-cook's answer
to the Indian takeaway

# lobster and avocado surprise

**Serves 8 ● 30-40 minutes to prepare**

**This sounds extraordinary, but is actually quite sensational and delicious, as well as psychedelic**

**What you need**
50g/2oz fresh strawberries
4 small (450g/1lb) boiled lobsters (to give
    about 300g/10$\frac{1}{2}$oz lobster meat)
2 ripe avocados
25g/1oz toasted flaked almonds

**Make sure you've got**
1 lemon
sunflower oil (150ml/$\frac{1}{4}$pint)

## ahead
❶ Make the dressing by hulling the strawberries and putting them in a food processor with the juice of half the lemon (save the rest for later), the oil and plenty of salt and pepper.
❷ Pick the lobster meat from the lobster shells and claws (unless you have an official lobster pick, a skewer helps). Refrigerate.

## at the last minute
❸ Halve the avocados and pull out the stones. Slice the flesh with the skin still on (and not cutting through the skin), then use a spatula to lever the flesh out – it should come away in neat slices.
❹ Arrange the pieces of lobster on a large serving plate, brighter side facing up, and nestle the avocado slices among them. Drizzle with the strawberry sauce and scatter with the almonds.

## make it your own You can serve this in the lobster shells – one each. Lay alternating slices of avocado and lobster in the shells and drizzle with the sauce.

# prawn, mango and spinach salad

**Serves 4 (easily halved or doubled)** ● **10-15 minutes to prepare (the mango and dressing can be prepared ahead, but assemble the dish at the table)**

**This glamorous main course salad has a distinctly Oriental feel.**

**What you need**
2 cm/¾in cube of fresh ginger, grated or
    finely chopped
half 225 g bag of young spinach leaves
200 g/7 oz shelled prawns, defrosted if frozen
1 large mango, peeled, stoned and thinly sliced
1 shallot or 2 spring onions, sliced very thinly

**Make sure you've got**
dry sherry (1 tbsp)
1 orange (finely grated zest and juice of ½ of it)
sunflower oil (3 tbsp)
toasted sesame oil (1 tsp)

## ahead
❶ Make the dressing by whisking the ginger, sherry, orange zest and juice, and the oils in a bowl. Season lightly.

## at the last minute
❷ When everyone is at the table, lay the spinach in a bowl and top with the prawns, mango and shallot or spring onions. Pour over the dressing and fold together gently.

You can buy pre-sliced mango, which saves a lot of slippery effort. You will need about 200g/7oz for this recipe.

## make it your own Shelled tiger prawns make the dish more luxurious. ● Use pawpaw (papaya) instead of mango.

# salmon with watercress mousseline

**Serves 6 (easily halved, or doubled for a large party)  ● 10-20 minutes to prepare**

**For this dish, you can buy poached salmon steaks, or even whole sides of salmon. Allow 125g/4oz per person.**

**What you need**
45g/1$\frac{1}{2}$oz watercress, plus a bouquet of
     beautiful sprigs to serve
125g/4oz fromage frais
6 poached salmon steaks or fillets (see above)

**Make sure you've got**
2 egg yolks
light olive oil or sunflower oil (100ml/3$\frac{1}{2}$fl oz)

## ahead
**❶** Put the watercress in a blender or processor and blitz to a smoothish purée. Add the egg yolks and, scraping down the sides as necessary, whiz to a green paste. With the machine running, start adding the oil, initially drop by drop, then in a thin stream. When all the oil is incorporated, stir or pulse in the fromage frais and season well. Transfer to a bowl.

## at the last minute
**❷** Put the salmon steaks on plates and generously spoon over the sauce. Add a top-knot of watercress to each plate and serve.

## make it your own Don't tell a soul, but adding 2 tsp of Pernod or Ricard to the sauce gives it a haunting herby flavour. No one will guess, but they will wonder what you've done.
● Instead of the watercress, you can halve a small tomato, discard the seeds and pulp, and cut the flesh into tiny dice. Dot this over the sauce and serve.

# smoked salmon and cucumber torte

**Serves 6-8 (excellent doubled for a grand affair) ● 30-40 minutes to prepare (but not much actual work)**

**This combination is rich and smart. Serve it in wedges with brown bread and butter, and lemon quarters.**

**What you need**
250g/9oz cucumber (1 small cucumber, or
    ½ a big one)
200ml/7floz crème fraîche, light or full-fat
plenty of chopped dill
200g/7oz sliced smoked salmon

**Make sure you've got**
1 lemon (finely grated zest and juice of)
horseradish sauce (2tsp)

## ahead

❶ To stop the cucumber becoming watery, peel it with a potato peeler, then cut it down the centre and scrape out the seeds of each half with a spoon. Slice each half in half again to make 4 long pieces, then slice these to about the thickness of a pound coin, or a bit thicker, and lay them on a piece of paper towel. Sprinkle with salt and leave for 15 minutes to an hour covered with more paper towel.

❷ Meanwhile, stand the ring of your smallest loose-bottomed cake tin (you won't need the base) on a plate to act as a mould.

❸ In a largish bowl, beat the crème fraîche, lemon zest, horseradish sauce and dill with plenty of black pepper. Crème fraîche varies and, if you are using full-fat, add 1-2 tbsp lemon juice to relax the cream, as you don't want it too stiff.

❹ Cut the salmon slices into ribbons about 2cm/$^3$/₄in across. It may be easiest to slice right through the salmon and any interleaving pieces of plastic film, but make sure you get rid of all the plastic. Then cut the ribbons at an angle into bite-size pieces.

❺ Rinse the cucumber to get rid of the salt and pat dry. Fold into the cream with the salmon pieces until well mixed, then spoon into the mould.

❻ Refrigerate for at least half an hour, or overnight if you wish.

## at the last minute

❼ Blot the plate with paper towels, if necessary. Run a knife round the edge of the cake tin and remove.

# shop & serve suppers

When you don't feel like cooking, there is no need to – just put together a clever combo of ingredients and enjoy an effortless tasty light meal. The following ideas are all generally intended for one, but are not too specific on quantities as you can vary these according to appetite, and easily scale them up to serve a couple or more.

1 **insalata tricolore** Scatter basil leaves over a platter and lay out buffalo mozzarella balls, fresh tomatoes and black olives. Drizzle with extra-virgin or basil-scented olive oil.

2 **avocado and feta salad** Peel and stone an avocado and cut in large chunks. Alternate on a serving plate with 85 g / 3 oz cubed feta and some black olives. Squeeze over lemon juice and eat with pitta bread.

3 **Italian ploughman's** Arrange 4 juicy plum tomatoes, a whole mozzarella and half a dozen balsamic-marinated baby onions on a plate. Drizzle with lemon-infused olive oil and mop up with ciabatta bread.

4 **ham with grapes and cheese toasts** Roll up slices of Serrano or other top-quality ham. Serve with seedless black grapes and slices of toast spread with cream or curd cheese.

5 **fig roll-ups** Cover ready-made pancakes with Parma or other good ham, scatter with Dolcelatte and fresh fig, both cut into small chunks, and rocket leaves. Drizzle with extra-virgin olive oil, roll tightly and slice in two.

LEFT prawn and mayonnaise leaves

BELOW Mediterranean vegetable platter

ABOVE goats' cheese with chicory and cherries

RIGHT gravlax with cucumber

**6** prawn and mayonnaise leaves   Lay out some Little Gem lettuce leaves and arrange on each some peeled cooked king prawns and a mini-dollop of mayo. Squeeze over lemon juice, snip over chives and eat.

**7** goats' cheese with chicory and cherries  Surround a fresh goats' cheese with crunchy chicory leaves. Sprinkle over and around some fresh cherries and eat the lot using a knife and your hands.

**8** Mediterranean vegetable platter  Drain 50g/2oz each of chargrilled peppers, artichokes and sun-blushed tomatoes and put on a plate. Snip over some basil leaves, squeeze over some lemon juice and enjoy with focaccia.

**9** gravlax with cucumber  Arrange narrow slices of gravlax (about 125g/4oz) and cucumber on a plate and drizzle over sour cream and chopped dill. Scoop up with buttered rye or German-style bread.

**10** pear and Stilton salad  Slice a fresh pear and 50g/2oz Stilton over lightly dressed watercress. Scatter with walnut halves and eat with a knife and fork.

# turkey tonnato

**Serves 4-6 ● 15-20 minutes to prepare**

**This is a variation on the classic Roman *vitello tonnato*, in which thin slices of veal are covered with smooth tuna mayonnaise. Poultry with fish may seem odd, but it's a sumptuous and very special dish.**

**What you need**

400g/14oz turkey from the delicatessen
   counter, thickly sliced (or two 190g packs
   of cooked skinless, boneless chicken
   breasts, i.e. 4 breasts)

**To decorate**

sliced olives
extra anchovies, rinsed and sliced
freshly chopped parsley

**Make sure you've got**

2 egg yolks
juice of ½ lemon
Dijon mustard (2 tsp)
sunflower oil (300ml/½ pint)
tuna in oil (200g/7oz), drained
3 anchovies, rinsed
capers (2 tbsp, plus more to decorate),
   rinsed

## ahead

❶ Make a mayonnaise by putting the egg yolks, lemon juice and mustard in the small bowl of your food processor. With the machine running, start adding the oil literally drop by drop; once the mix starts to look thick and gloopy, add the oil in a thin stream.

❷ When all the oil is incorporated, add the tuna, anchovies and capers, and whiz until smooth. Taste and season – it may need a little more lemon juice, plus pepper and possibly salt. It may also need a little water to get a good spreading consistency.

❸ Cut the turkey into slices about the size of a five-pound note; if using chicken, slice the chicken breasts in 3 laterally.

❹ Spread a spatula of the mayonnaise over a large, flat serving plate. Selecting the less well-shaped slices, arrange half the turkey in one layer on the mayonnaise.

❺ Spread with half the remaining mayo, then arrange the remaining turkey slices on top, like the blades of a propeller. Finish by covering everything with the remaining mayo.

## at the last minute

❻ Decorate with the capers, olives and anchovies, then dust generously with parsley.

# fruity almond chicken (simple)

**Serves 4 (easily multiplied) ● 10-20 minutes to prepare**

**Pretty, stylish and very tasty, this is a great dish for a summer lunch party.**

**What you need**
400g/14oz cooked skinless and boneless
    chicken breasts (about 4 breasts)
4 spring onions, shredded
50g pack of crispy fried bacon
50g/2oz roasted unsalted almonds, halved
snipped chives

**Make sure you've got**
mayonnaise (125ml/4fl oz), bought or
    home-made, see page 87)
2 oranges
2 bananas

## ahead
❶ Segment the oranges by peeling them completely, then cutting each segment
free of its membrane. Do this over a bowl to catch the juice, drop the segments
into the bowl as you free them and squeeze any juice remaining in the membranes
afterwards with your hand.
❷ Peel the bananas and slice them at angle into the orange juice. Turn them to
make sure they are completely coated.
❸ Slice the chicken into bite-sized strips and add to the bowl with the spring onions.
Crumble in the bacon, then fold in the mayonnaise to coat everything. Chill for an
hour or two.

## at the last minute
❹ Transfer the contents of the bowl to a serving dish and sprinkle with the nuts and
chives to serve.

## make it your own You can also make this dish with cooked turkey. If you buy it from
the delicatessen counter, ask them to slice it very thickly, preferably by hand, so it ends up
sufficiently chunky.

# smoked chicken with red pepper sauce

**Serves 6-8 (perfect to multiply for larger numbers) ● 30-40 minutes to prepare**

**Look for smoked chickens in good delicatessens – they are good to keep in your freezer.**

**What you need**
1 smoked chicken, about 1.2 kg / 2 lb 10 oz
50 g / 2 oz firm goats' cheese
handful of parsley
25 g / 1 oz walnut pieces, chopped

**for the dressing**
50 g / 2 oz marinated or chargrilled red peppers
125 ml / 4 fl oz fromage frais or sour cream

**to serve**
150 g / 5 oz black grapes, halved and deseeded
    if necessary

## ahead
❶ Skin the chicken and remove the flesh from the carcass, including wings and legs.
❷ Put 125 g / 4 oz of the chicken (using the shredded scraps from wings and carcass rather than the meat from the breast) in a processor and whiz with the goats' cheese and parsley until smooth. Transfer to a bowl and mix in the walnuts (this stops the walnuts getting obliterated while processing the other ingredients).
❸ Season and pile on to a large square of cling film. Roll the cling film up to shape the mixture into a 10 cm / 4 in sausage, packing it firmly together. Put in the fridge and leave for a couple of hours, or up to a day.
❹ Up to 4 hours before you want to serve, slice the remaining chicken as neatly as possible, cover and set aside.
❺ Make the dressing by whizzing the peppers and fromage frais or soured cream in a food processor until smooth. Check and adjust the seasoning.

## at the last minute
❻ Arrange the chicken on a large serving plate and drizzle with the sauce. Unwrap the sausage of smoked chicken and walnut mousse and cut into thick discs with a sharp knife. Top the sliced chicken with the discs of mousse and scatter with grapes.

## make it your own This looks classy on individual plates. Top the chicken and sauce with a single slice of the mousse plus a scattering of grapes.

smoked chicken with red pepper sauce

# chicken and walnut salad *(simple)*

**Serves 2 (easily halved)** ● **10-15 minutes to prepare**

**What you need**

200g/7oz cooked chicken breast, skinless
    and boneless, cut into strips

4 cherry tomatoes, quartered

1 spring onion, chopped

50g/2oz walnuts, chopped

1 tbsp sour cream

small handful of mint

**Make sure you've got**

olive oil (2 tbsp)

wine vinegar (1 tsp)

Dijon mustard (1 tsp)

❶ Put the chicken, tomatoes, spring onions and walnuts in a bowl and mix lightly.

❷ Make the dressing by whisking the oil with the vinegar, then whisking in the mustard and sour cream.

❸ Fold the salad and dressing together, and scatter thickly with the mint.

# spicy chicken paprika

**Serves 2** ● **10-20 minutes to prepare**

**What you need**

125g/4oz fromage frais, plus a little extra

35g/1$\frac{1}{4}$oz chargrilled or marinated peppers,
    sliced

1 celery stalk, chopped

200g/7oz cooked chilli chicken, sliced into
    bite-sized pieces

2 ready-to-eat poppadums

**Make sure you've got**

chutney (1 tbsp)

smoked paprika ($\frac{1}{2}$tsp)

squeeze of lemon juice, if you like

❶ Make the sauce by mixing 100g/3$\frac{1}{2}$oz fromage frais with the peppers, chutney, celery and paprika. The mixture should not need any extra seasoning. Stir in the sliced chicken.

❷ Pile on the poppadums and top with fromage frais. Some lemon juice adds zing.

# Circassian chicken

**Serves 4 (easily halved or multiplied)** ● **10-20 minutes to prepare (make ahead)**

**In this Turkish salad, chicken is smothered in a bread and walnut sauce.**

**What you need**
4 cooked skinless and boneless chicken
    breasts, each about 100g/3½oz
125g/4oz walnuts
freshly chopped tarragon, to finish (optional)

**Make sure you've got**
boiling water (225ml/8fl oz)
good-quality vegetable bouillon powder, such as
    Marigold (1 tsp)
fresh white bread, crusts removed (60g/2½oz)
walnut oil (1 tbsp)
paprika (¾tsp)

## ahead

❶ Cut each chicken breast at an angle across the grain into 5-6 slices, keeping them separate.

❷ In small bowl, pour the boiling water over the bouillon powder and mix well. Process the walnuts with the bread and add enough of the bouillon mixture to make a sloppy paste.

❸ Reassemble each of the chicken breasts on a shallow serving dish or plate, slice by slice and with a teaspoon of the sauce between each slice. When all the breasts are reassembled, spoon over remaining sauce to mask them completely. Leave for at least half an hour or up to 4 hours. Mix the walnut oil and paprika together.

## at the last minute

❹ If any liquid has leaked from the sauce, blot with paper towel. Drizzle with the red walnut oil and serve sprinkled with tarragon if you wish.

# Jubilee chicken (simple)

**Serves 6 ● 20-30 minutes to prepare**

**Invented for the Queen's Golden Jubilee, this is a fresh take on coronation chicken.**

**What you need**

600g/1lb 5oz cooked skinless and boneless chicken breasts (6 breasts)

350g/12oz fresh cherries

two 85g bags of watercress

4-5 spring onions, shredded

200g/7oz fromage frais

small handful of mint, finely chopped, to finish

**Make sure you've got**

curry paste (1 tbsp, see note on page 14)

honey (1 tsp)

½ lemon

## ahead

❶ Cut the chicken into bite-sized pieces. Stone the cherries – or better still, get someone to do it for you.

❷ Layer up the ingredients in your serving dish: first the watercress, then the chicken, next the cherries and finally the spring onions.

## at the last minute

❸ Make the dressing by whisking together the fromage frais, curry paste, honey and 1 tbsp lemon juice. Season to taste and drizzle over the salad. Finally, sprinkle the salad with mint.

# devilled chicken and avocado salad

**Serves 4 (easily halved or doubled)** ● **15-25 minutes preparation (depending on whether you've bought chicken already skinned and boned)**

**What you need**

100 ml carton of half-fat crème fraîche

half 225g bag of young spinach leaves

450g/1 lb cooked chicken (about ½ medium
    roast chicken) on the bone or
    300g/10½ oz off

2 ripe tomatoes, white cores removed, cut into
    thin wedges, seeds and pulp discarded

1 avocado, peeled and cut into thin strips

**Make sure you've got**

1 garlic clove, crushed

Dijon mustard (2 tsp)

tomato ketchup (2 tsp)

Tabasco sauce (good splash of)

Worcestershire sauce (good splash of)

smoked paprika, for dusting

## ahead

❶ Make the dressing by whisking the crème fraîche, garlic, mustard, ketchup and sauces together. Adjust the seasoning, if necessary.

## at the last minute

❷ Put the spinach in a large bowl, season and toss with one-third of the dressing. Arrange on a serving dish. Add the remaining ingredients except the paprika and the rest of the dressing to the just-vacated bowl, stir and toss them on top of the spinach. Dust with smoked paprika.

**Hass avocados, often from South Africa, are the wrinkly black-skinned ones. They have the advantage of not going brown, once cut, for up to 2 hours. The way to get the peel off is to halve them lengthwise and twist the halves to separate. Don't peel at this point – instead, slice the flesh or cut it in squares (without cutting through the skin), then run a rubber spatula between flesh and skin and pop out the cubes of flesh.**

# Marsala chicken with sultanas (simple)

**Serves 4 ● 10-15 minutes to prepare (make an hour or two, or even up to a day, ahead)**

**This simple dish is elegant and understated.**

**What you need**
2 tbsp Marsala
two 190g packs of cooked skinless and
   boneless chicken breast (4 breasts)

**Make sure you've got**
sultanas or seedless raisins (50g/2oz)
$1/2$ orange (finely grated zest of)
boiling water
balsamic vinegar (2 tsp)
olive oil (4 tbsp)

## ahead
❶ Put the sultanas or raisins and orange zest in a small bowl and pour over boiling water to cover. Leave for at least 10 minutes and up to an hour. Drain, reserving the sultanas and orange zest.
❷ Whisk the Marsala and vinegar with seasoning to taste and then whisk in the oil until well blended into a sauce. Add the reserved sultanas and orange zest.
❸ Slice the chicken neatly and thinly. Arrange on a serving dish and pour over the sauce. Leave at room temperature and then serve, or chill overnight (bring back to room temperature to serve).

This needs a very plain accompaniment, such as couscous. If also serving a salad, bring it out after the main course, as a vinegary dressing will spoil the sweetness of the sauce.

Balsamic vinegar varies: the oldest and best is slightly thick and very sweet; supermarket brands can be thin and more like soy sauce. If you have only the latter, taste carefully and add less balsamic vinegar, or extra sugar, if necessary.

## make it your own
Instead of the Marsala, you can use sweet sherry, sweet white wine or even dry white wine with $1/2$ tsp sugar dissolved in it. ● You can use lemon zest instead of orange. In the original Italian recipe, candied lemon zest is used, but I find this a bit fruitcaky for modern tastes.

# warm three-cheese salad *(simple)*

**Serves 4 (easily halved or doubled)** ● **10-15 minutes to prepare**

**What you need**

two 50g bag of rocket leaves

2 ripe pears, peeled and each sliced into
    8 slim wedges

150g/5oz good ripe Brie

125g/4oz firm goats' cheese (such as
    Capricorn)

50g/2oz walnuts, roughly chopped

125g/4oz grated Double Gloucester or
    Cheddar cheese

1 punnet of mustard and cress

**Make sure you've got**

squeeze of lemon juice

olive oil (2 tbsp)

walnut oil (2 tbsp)

sherry vinegar, red wine vinegar or
    balsamic vinegar (2 tsp)

## ahead

❶ Layer up the salad in a large bowl, seasoning lightly with a little salt and plenty of black pepper as you go. Start with the rocket, then fan the pear slices (which you have dipped lightly in lemon juice) out over this, followed by the Brie (cut into cubes) and the goats' cheese (cut into thin slices). Scatter with walnuts and the grated cheese, then snip over the mustard and cress.

## at the last minute

❷ Heat the oils and vinegar in a microwave or small pan until boiling, whisk and pour over the salad. Toss and serve at once.

## make it your own This salad can be infinitely varied. The essential components are a soft cheese, a firmer cheese and a hard cheese in any combination. If you are patriotic, go for a British Brie, with Capricorn (from Somerset) and any of our fine English hard cheeses. For an Italian feel, go for Dolcelatte, Taleggio and Parmesan for grating.

# eastern supper

**Serves 4 - easily halved or doubled ● 20-30 minutes to prepare**

**This feast of lovely dishes – only one of which needs cooking – is the equivalent of a vegetarian curry supper and gives an engaging banquet feeling.**

**What you need**

**for the peach relish**

2 fresh peaches

5 cm / 1 inch of fresh ginger, peeled and finely chopped

4 spring onions, shredded

**for the coriander yoghurt**

142 ml / ¼ pint carton of Greek yoghurt

handful of coriander, chopped

juice of ½ lime

**for the couscous**

squeeze of lime juice

**for the vegetables**

400 g / 14 oz antipasto vegetables – red peppers, aubergine, artichokes, sun-dried tomatoes, olives, all sliced or roughly chopped

**Make sure you've got**

red wine vinegar (2 tsp)

couscous (250 g / 9 oz)

olive oil (1 tbsp)

curry paste (1 tbsp)

200 ml / 7 fl oz boiling water

**1** Make the peach relish: score the peach skin into quarters, pour over boiling water to cover generously and, after 30 seconds, lift out with a fork and remove the skin. Chop the flesh and stir together with the ginger, spring onions and vinegar.
**2** Make the coriander yoghurt by mixing all the ingredients together, adding a pinch of salt.
**3** Make the couscous by putting it into a bowl with the oil. Put the curry paste into a measuring jug, add the boiling water and pour over couscous. Add the lime juice and leave for 10 minutes, stirring occasionally.
**4** Prepare the vegetables by piling them into a sieve and rinsing them under cold running water. Slice roughly.
**5** To serve, stir the vegetables into the couscous and serve with the accompaniments.

a shopping hint  Check out the small print on your curry paste – some makes need to be cooked to use. If that is the case, stir-fry it for a minute or two, or sizzle in a small dish in the microwave, covered with cling film.

make it your own  For a more substantial feast (for meat eaters) you can add to the mêlée one or two 200g packs of tikka masala cooked turkey fillets.

eastern supper

# stylish
# side dishes

save valuable time with imaginative no-cook accompaniments;
some refreshing, some unusual, but all inspired and certain
to complement the range of no-cook main courses

# chicory in the Belgian style

**Serves 2 (easily multiplied)** ● **10-20 minutes to prepare**

**What you need**

2 heads of chicory, trimmed, cored and cut
    into bite-sized chunks

14g/$^1/_2$oz (4 little squares) white chocolate

1 dsp beer or lager, ideally Belgian

snipped chives, to serve

**Make sure you've got**

olive oil (1 dsp)

Dijon mustard (1 tsp)

❶ Deal with the chicory at the last minute as it goes brown immediately.
❷ Melt the chocolate in the microwave or over hot water, then whisk in the beer
until smooth. While still whisking, add the oil, mustard and seasoning.
❸ Drizzle this over the chicory, scatter with chopped chives and serve.

# real Greek salad (simple)

**Serves 4 (easily halved or doubled)** ● **10-20 minutes to prepare**

**What you need**

4 large tomatoes, seeds and pulp discarded, diced

6cm/$2^1/_2$in cucumber, peeled, deseeded
    and diced

2 celery stalks, diced

1 yellow pepper, deseeded and diced

12-16 green or red olives, pitted and roughly
    chopped

2 spring onions, shredded

250g/9oz feta in oil, cut into 1cm/$^1/_2$in cubes

handful of mint, chopped

**Make sure you've got**

extra-virgin olive oil (4 tbsp)

lemon juice (4 tsp)

❶ Mix together all the vegetables, with the cheese and mint.
❷ Mix the oil and lemon juice to make a dressing and fold into the salad. Season to
taste. Serve at once or chill, and then bring back to room temperature to serve.

# Vietnamese coleslaw

**Serves 4 ● 15-20 minutes to prepare**

**Here unusual flavours take coleslaw to new heights.**

**What you need**
3 spring onions
½ small white cabbage
1 large carrot
couple of celery stalks, or 1 fennel bulb
50g bag of salted peanuts (not dry-roasted)

**Make sure you've got**
1 small red chilli
peanut butter (2 tbsp)
mayonnaise (4 tbsp)
soy sauce (good splash)

## ahead
❶ Shred the spring onions and deseed and finely chop the chilli. Very thinly slice the cabbage, carrot and celery, either on a grater, in the food processor or by hand. Mix all these together in a big bowl.
❷ In a small bowl, whisk together the peanut butter, mayo and soy sauce. Fold this dressing into the coleslaw. No added salt and pepper are necessary.
❸ Sprinkle in the peanuts and serve.

## make it your own
You can build this into more of a main course by adding one or two skinned and shredded cooked chicken breasts. Vegetarians can add Quorn, sliced into strips. Rice crackers make a nice accompaniment.

# dressing to impress

When making salad dressings, there are many tempting oils and vinegars to choose from. Olive oil and extra-virgin olive oil are, of course, the automatic choice for Mediterranean-type dishes, but otherwise I use sunflower. New-kid-on-the-block argan oil, from Morocco, is nutty and mild, with an attractive greenish hue. Nut oils (especially sesame) are best used with equal parts sunflower as they are strong (in the case of toasted sesame, a few drops will do). Some flavoured vinegars are sweet, especially fruit and flower ones, and you need add no sugar. Rice wine vinegar is great for Oriental-type salads. If I want a lemony taste, I usually add a little finely grated zest or a very little juice, as too much juice cam make a dressing acid.

**1** make your own mayo Bought mayonnaise is great, but home-made is even better. I don't use olive oil as this makes it bitter. For classic mayonnaise, put 2–3 egg yolks, 1 dessertspoon Dijon mustard, a squeeze of lemon juice and some seasoning in a blender or processor. Start adding 300–450 ml / $^1/_2$–$^3/_4$ pint sunflower oil, drop by drop, gradually increasing the speed until you are adding it in a thin stream. Taste, and stop adding oil when the eggy taste has gone, but before it starts to taste oily. I add 1–3 tbsp boiling water at this point to make the texture more light and whippy.

**2** cheat's mayo It's not exactly cheating, but you can make brilliant mayo with a stick blender and the tall narrow jug that comes with it. Put 1 whole egg, 150 ml / $^1/_4$ pint sunflower oil, 1 dessertspoon Dijon mustard, salt, pepper and a squeeze of lemon juice in the jug. Put the blender right to the bottom, over the egg, and switch on. After a few seconds, very slowly start to lift the stick blender. Hey presto!

**3** avocado-aise Make a lighter, fresher mayonnaise by processing 1 egg yolk, the flesh of $^1/_2$ avocado, mustard, lemon juice and seasoning, with 150 ml - 300 ml / $^1/_4$ - $^1/_2$ pint sunflower oil in the same way as classic mayonnaise above.

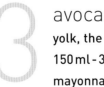

**4** season your salad, not your dressing With a leaf salad, put the salt and pepper on the leaves, not in the dressing. Lightly tumble the leaves about in the salad bowl with the seasoning, then dress.

**5 give yourself some space** Don't try and toss your salad in too small a bowl – either you won't do the job properly or it will go everywhere (or both). If your serving bowl is small, toss the salad in a big bowl, then transfer to the serving bowl. If there are only two of you and you are using a bagged salad, you can put the dressing in the bag and lightly shake, then transfer directly to plates.

**6 whisking is the secret** One secret of a great dressing is to emulsify the oil and vinegar well, as this blends the flavours and gives a silky coating to salad ingredients. A micro-whisk or mini-balloon whisk is better than a fork or shaking in a jar.

**7 sea salt and freshly ground black pepper** Grind your own sea salt – Maldon salt, or the French fleur de sel – using a pestle and mortar, and add by the pinch. The flavour is finer and cleaner. Always grind black peppercorns fresh, and, for more impact, add a pinch of crushed chill-

**8 good for you** Salads that include citrus fruit, like grapefruit, may need no dressing at all – let the juice do the work. If using lemon juice in a dress-ing, remember that too much can make it acid – boost the lemon flavour with some finely grated zest.Rice wine vinegar is mild enough to be used without oil. Whisk flavourings into fromage frais for a creamy dressing without fat.

**9 the winning formula** Everyone's taste differs, but I use 3 tbsp oil to 2 tsp vinegar for a salad for 3-4 people. I usually add 1–2 tsp Dijon mustard and a pinch of sugar, and simply put everything into a small bowl and whisk until combined.

**10 dressing too strong?** If you generally find dressings too strong, you can use a French trick: whisk 1 tbsp of water into a French dressing. This slows the speed at which the vinegar hits the palate, and rounds out the flavour without diluting it.

LEFT give yourself some space

BELOW sea salt and freshly ground black pepper

ABOVE whisking is the secret

RIGHT good for you

# a trio of Moroccan salads (simple)

These are all best served at room temperature, accompanied by flat breads ● Each salad serves 2, but if you make all three you will have enough for 4-6 ● Tomato and beetroot take 5-10 minutes to prepare, the carrot 15-20 minutes

## tomato and lemon

**What you need**

2 ripe juicy medium-sized tomatoes

1 miniature preserved lemon, seeds removed
    and very thinly sliced

**Make sure you've got**

ground cumin ($\frac{1}{2}$ tsp)

extra-virgin olive oil or argan oil (1 tbsp)

sugar

❶  Halve the tomatoes and discard their seeds and pulp. Slice them thinly.

❷  Mix with the cumin, preserved lemon, oil, plenty of seasoning and a pinch of sugar.

## beetroot and rosewater

**What you need**

125g/4oz cooked baby beetroot

**Make sure you've got**

rosewater (1 tbsp)

extra-virgin olive oil or argan oil (1 tbsp)

❶  Cut each beetroot into 6 tiny wedges.

❷  Mix with the rosewater and oil, and season well.

## carrot and harissa

**What you need**

2 carrots, peeled

**Make sure you've got**

boiling water

harissa paste (1 tsp)

extra-virgin olive oil or argan oil (2 tsp)

$\frac{1}{2}$ lemon

❶  Cut the carrots into matchsticks as small as patience will allow. Put these in a heatproof bowl. Pour over boiling water to cover and blanch for 5 minutes, then drain and refresh in cold water. Drain again and pat dry on paper towel.

❷  Mix with the harissa, oil and plenty of salt and pepper. Squeeze over some lemon juice just before serving.

# succotash salad (simple)

**Serves 4-6 ● 10-20 minutes to prepare**

**This colourful jumble of fresh goodness is based on a Native American dish. In American style, use the can the sweetcorn comes in as a measure for the other ingredients.**

**What you need**

285g can of sweetcorn, drained

1 canful of frozen broad beans

1 canful of finely diced courgette (1 small
    courgette)

$\frac{1}{2}$ canful of finely diced cucumber

1 canful of deseeded tomatoes (about 3 medium
    tomatoes), cut into strips

2 spring onions, shredded

2 large slices of chargrilled pepper (such as
    Spanish piquillo), sliced

10 mint leaves, finely chopped

**Make sure you've got**

boiling water

1 garlic clove, crushed

sunflower oil (2 tbsp)

white wine vinegar (2 tsp)

## ahead

❶ Empty the corn into a big bowl, and use the can to measure the beans and courgette into another bowl. Pour boiling water over the vegetables and leave for 5 minutes to blanch, then drain.

❷ Mix the blanched vegetables into the corn, together with the cucumber, tomatoes, spring onions and pepper. Season well.

❸ Make the dressing by mixing (either by hand or in a processor) the garlic, mint, oil and vinegar. Pour it over the salad and chill until ready to serve.

## at the last minute

❹ Adjust the seasoning if necessary. If the salad has been standing for more than a few minutes, transfer with a slotted spoon to a fresh bowl, leaving behind the juices.

**This is a great salad for a party. Scale it up for 8 by using a large can of corn, or multiply.**

# pear, beetroot and Stilton salad (simple)

**Serves 4 as a side dish or starter (easily halved)** ● 10-15 minutes to prepare

**What you need**

2 pears, peeled and each sliced into 8 wedges

225g/8oz cooked beetroot, sliced into 8 wedges

100g/4oz Stilton, cut into small cubes

100ml/3$\frac{1}{2}$fl oz light or full-fat crème fraîche

**Make sure you've got**

balsamic vinegar (1 tsp)

## ahead

❶ On a shallow serving dish, fan out alternating pear and beetroot wedges.

❷ Lightly mix together the Stilton, crème fraîche and vinegar.

## at the last minute

❸ Season the pears and beetroot with pepper and drizzle the sauce over them. Toss and serve.

# orange three-bean salad (simple)

**Serves 4 (easily halved or doubled)** ● 10-20 minutes to prepare

**What you need**

225g/8oz frozen broad beans

400g can of chickpeas, rinsed and drained

400g can of black beans, rinsed and drained

snipped chives or chopped parsley, to finish

**Make sure you've got**

boiling water

rice wine vinegar (1 dsp)

finely grated zest of $\frac{1}{2}$ orange and 1 dsp juice

freshly grated ginger (2 tsp)

sunflower oil (5 tbsp)

toasted sunflower oil (few drops, optional)

❶ Put the broad beans in a bowl with $\frac{1}{2}$tsp salt, pour over lots of boiling water and leave for 5-10 minutes. Drain, put back in the bowl, cover with cold water to chill quickly, then drain again. Mix with the chickpeas and black beans.

❷ Mix together all the remaining ingredients except the herbs. Mix into the salad, then fold in the herbs.

# lentil and radish salad *(simple)*

**Serves 4 ● 10-15 minutes to prepare**

**What you need**
16 radishes
big handful of parsley, finely chopped
400g can of green or brown lentils, rinsed
    and drained

**Make sure you've got**
caraway seeds (1 tbsp)
2 garlic cloves, finely chopped
sherry vinegar (1 tbsp)
whole-grain mustard (3 tbsp)
extra-virgin olive oil (5 tbsp)

## ahead
❶ Roughly crush the caraway seeds using a pestle and mortar. If you've got one of those big Jamie Oliver-style ones, add the garlic and mash that too – and make the dressing in the mortar; otherwise, make the dressing in a bowl.
❷ Whisk in the vinegar, mustard and seasoning, followed by the oil, to make a dressing.

## at the last minute
❸ Roughly chop the radishes and finely chop the parsley. Fold these into the lentils with the dressing.

# cucumber with poppy seeds *(simple)*

**Serves 4 ● 5-10 minutes to prepare**

**What you need**
400g / 14oz cucumber (1 small cucumber)

**Make sure you've got**
$1/2$ red chilli, very finely chopped
poppy seeds (2 tsp)
rice wine vinegar ($1^1/2$ tsp)

❶ Peel the cucumber and halve it down the centre. Drag a spoon down the centre to scrape away the seeds and discard them. Slice the cucumber across into crescents and put in a serving bowl.
❷ Scatter over the chilli, poppy seeds and vinegar, and serve.

# tomato tabouleh

**Serves 6 ● 15-20 minutes to prepare (thanks to the food processor)**

**What you need**

225g/8oz bulgur wheat (not the coarse kind)

large handful of parsley

small handful of mint

1 large carrot, peeled and quartered

1 large green pepper, quartered

300ml can of V8 vegetable juice

**Make sure you've got**

1 onion

1 lemon (juice of)

extra-virgin olive oil (3 tbsp)

## ahead

❶ Bulgur wheat can need rinsing; if in doubt, rinse it in a sieve. Tip it into a large bowl.

❷ Chop the herbs finely and add to the bulgur. Do the same with each vegetable.

❸ Stir in the remaining ingredients with 200ml/7fl oz water and $\frac{1}{2}$ tsp salt, and leave in the fridge overnight.

## at the last minute

❹ Bring to room temperature and drain off any liquid not absorbed before serving.

# jewelled couscous

**Serves 2 (easily doubled) ● 10-20 minutes to prepare**

**What you need**

125g/4oz couscous

1 tbsp dried cranberries

2 fresh dates, finely chopped

1 fresh apricot, finely chopped

fresh coriander leaves, chopped

**Make sure you've got**

good-quality vegetable bouillon powder,
    preferably Marigold (1 tsp)

olive oil (1 tbsp, optional)

boiling water (200ml/7fl oz)

❶ Put the couscous in a bowl with the bouillon powder, cranberries and oil, if using.

❷ Pour over the boiling water and leave for 10 minutes, stirring occasionally.

❸ Stir in the fresh fruit. Add the coriander and season. Fluff again to serve.

something on the side

**To fill that potato-shaped space, instead of buying expensive – and not always very nice – potato salads and the like, try some of these wonderfully nutty, healthy grains or satisfying noodles that only require soaking in boiling water.**

COUSCOUS The staple of North Africa is a storecupboard must. Put 250g/9oz in a bowl, cover with 450ml/$^3$/$_4$pint boiling water with some seasoning, and leave for a minimum of 10 minutes, stirring occasionally with a fork. Finely grated lemon or lime zest and juice, freshly grated ginger, soy sauce and other flavourings can be added with the water. Chopped herbs can be forked in just before serving.

herby lemon couscous Plain couscous is a good foil for other flavours, but I usually add 1$^1$/$_2$tsp good-quality vegetable bouillon powder, like Marigold, in place of seasoning, the juice of $^1$/$_2$ lemon and 1 tbsp extra-virgin olive (or a flavoured) oil. Finish by forking in freshly chopped mint, coriander or parsley.

tabouleh To make this classic Arabian salad for 4–6, put 175g/6oz bulgur in a bowl and mix with the juice of a lemon, plenty of salt, pepper and a pinch of cayenne, a chopped tomato, 2 shredded spring onions, 2 tbsp olive oil and a large handful each of parsley and mint (the volume of chopped herbs should be greater than the volume of bulgur). Pour over 450ml/$^3$/$_4$pint water and leave for half an hour. Squeeze out any excess liquid, adjust the seasoning and serve.

bulgur wheat Not found in every supermarket, but you'll get it in health-food shops. For no-cooking, you need finely ground bulgur, not coarse (if not specified, it's likely to be fine – looking like Demerara sugar). Simply add water (quantity isn't critical, but I use 175g/6oz bulgur to 450ml/$^3$/$_4$pint liquid) and leave for at least half an hour for the grain to swell. Squeeze out excess liquid. Lots of herbs, flavourings and seasoning are called for – add with the water.

barley couscous One up on plain couscous, this has more flavour, a slightly darker colour and a slightly more chewy consistency. Make it in just the same way.

**6** Chinese egg noodles Usually sold as 'instant noodles', these are indispensable for no-cooking. They have a good firm consistency and are already seasoned, so enhance most dishes. Avoid flavoured varieties, which have an artificial taste. Packet instructions usually tell you to boil them for 2 minutes, but I get perfect results by putting them in a heatproof bowl (do not add salt) and covering with boiling water. Leave for 10 minutes, stirring occasionally. Check they're tender; if not, leave a little longer. If you're going to incorporate the noodles into other ingredients, break them up a bit before adding the boiling water – this makes them less tangly and easier to mix in.

**7** savoury noodles To serve noodles as a side dish, splash soy, sweet chilli or teriyaki sauce over instant noodles.

**8** rice noodles As fast and convenient as Chinese egg noodles, these are more suited to delicate Thai flavours. Those usually on sale here are wide and flat – like fettuccine. Sprinkle $1/2$ tsp salt over them in the heatproof bowl, cover with boiling water, then leave for 4-6 minutes or according to packet instructions. Don't prepare until you need them, or they stick together. They're also inclined to tangle, so if they are to be mixed with other ingredients snap them in pieces.

**9** Thai stir-fry noodles Also known as stick noodles or rice sticks, these come in tiny sheaves, a bit like doll's-house spaghetti. As with the broader rice noodles, leave these in salted boiling water for 4 minutes, and don't make ahead. When combining with other ingredients, fold in a few at a time or layer.

**10** vermicelli This most light and delicate member of the pasta family doesn't need cooking. Treat like Oriental noodles – put in a bowl with salt and cover with boiling water. After 10 minutes, drain and use. Vermicelli will break up if you mix it with other ingredients, so layer it instead.

**LEFT** fine rice noodles or rice sticks

**BELOW** dried egg noodles soaking in boiling water

**RIGHT** broad rice noodles or rice sticks

**FAR RIGHT** nests of fine egg noodles

as long as it is balanced, no-cooking can, by its very nature, be incredibly good for you, as it relies so heavily on nutritious raw vegetables and fruit. If you are counting carbs and fat, these recipes have nutritional analyses

# deliciously healthy

# fruits of the forest thickie *(simple)*

**Serves 2 (or 2 indulgent drinks for one deserving person) ● 5 minutes to prepare**

**What you need**
250g/9oz frozen fruits of the forest
1 banana
300-450ml/½-¾pint yoghurt

**Make sure you've got**
honey or maple syrup (2-3tsp)

❶ Whiz the fruits of the forest in a food processor until finely chopped.
❷ Add the banana and whiz again. Scrape down the sides, then add the honey or syrup and enough yoghurt to make your preferred sweetness and consistency. It is impossible to be too dogmatic, as fruit and yoghurt vary so much.
❸ Transvase into long glasses and drink in the health.

make it your own The formula is identical for other fruit drinks. Put in the main fruit (fresh or frozen) before the other ingredients and make sure it is thoroughly blitzed. ● Strawberries, raspberries, blackberries, blueberries, mango and pineapple are all good. Or use a mixture of two - not more than two, or the taste will be lost. ● Follow your tastebuds and add a sprig of mint at stage 1, or 3 drops of vanilla extract. If it is too thick for your taste, dilute it with orange or apple juice. ● On a really hot day, make ice cubes out of fruit juice and use to cool the thickies.

per serving Energy 166 kcalories, protein 9.2g, carbohydrate 30.2g, fat 1.8g, saturated fat 1.0g, fibre 3.6g, added sugars none, salt 0.33g ● Super-healthy; good source of calcium and vitamin C; very low in calories and fat; counts as 2 of your 5-a-day.

# avocado and grapefruit salad

**Serves 2 ● 10-15 minutes to prepare**

**Think California here for this beautiful fresh zingy salad of enormous delicacy, inspired by American chef Alice Waters. It is enough to convert the most confirmed grapefruit hater.**

**What you need**
2 medium-sized pink grapefruits
4 spring onions, shredded
small bag of rocket
1 ripe avocado, peeled, stoned and cut into
    thin slices
chives, to snip over

**Make sure you've got**
wine vinegar or sherry vinegar (2 tsp)
extra-virgin olive oil (5 tbsp)

❶ Segment the grapefruit as described below. Put the segments in a bowl and squeeze over the juice from the membranes and pith. Lift out the segments and mix with the spring onions.

❷ Remove 1 tbsp of the grapefruit juice (drink or save the rest) and put in a small bowl. Whisk with the vinegar, oil and seasoning.

❸ Toss the rocket lightly with 1 tbsp of this dressing and arrange on 2 plates.

❹ Top with the grapefruit and avocado and drizzle over the dressing. Snip over chives.

If you've never segmented an orange or grapefruit, it's a trick worth knowing as the fruit is so delicious prepared this way. First get your knife good and sharp. Peel off all the skin and pith with the knife, then slice each individual segment free of its membrane, so it pops out easily, gradually leaving a fan of the tough membranes. Do this over a bowl to catch the juice.

## per serving
Energy 400 kcalories, protein 4.6g, carbohydrate 15.1g, fat 36.0g, saturated fat 4.7g, fibre 5.7g, added sugars none, salt 0.04g. ● Super-healthy; although high in overall fat content because of the avocado and the oil, low in saturated fat and salt; good source of folic acid and vitamin C; counts as 2 of your 5-a-day.

# chicken with pink grapefruit and sweetcorn

**Serves 2 ● 20-25 minutes to prepare**

**This salad is light, pretty and deliciously fresh.**

**What you need**
225g/8oz cooked chicken, skinless and
   boneless
1 corn on the cob, or a 285g can of sweetcorn,
   drained
1 pink grapefruit

**Make sure you've got**
boiling water
$1/2$ red chilli

❶ Slice the chicken and put in a bowl.
❷ Strip the kernels off the cob into another bowl (stand it on end and cut right down with a heavy knife at several points all round) and pour over boiling water. Leave for 5 minutes, then drain and add to the chicken. If using canned, just drain.
❸ Peel the grapefruit with a knife and segment it as described on page 105, holding it in your hand and rotating it as you go. Add the segments to the chicken. Again using your hand, squeeze the juice from the membranes over the chicken and discard them.
❹ Deseed the chilli and chop it finely, then stir it in and season well. The salad can be eaten at once or chilled. Simple couscous makes a good accompaniment.

per serving Energy 201 kcalories, protein 27.2g, carbohydrate 18.5g, fat 2.4g, saturated fat 0.4g, fibre 2.3g, added sugars none, salt 0.16g. ● Super-healthy; very low in fat and added sugars; good source of folic acid and vitamin C; counts as 2 of your 5-a-day.

# chunky fresh tomato soup

**Serves 6 (serve with bread for a main course) ● 10-20 minutes to prepare**

**Use the best ripe tomatoes you can find. Out of season, it helps to add a dash of tomato purée to improve the colour of the soup.**

**What you need**
8 juicy ripe medium-sized tomatoes
1 small red onion, roughly chopped
good handful of fresh coriander, plus extra to serve
500g carton of passata (crushed tomatoes)
400g can of cannellini beans or butter beans, drained
tortilla chips, to serve

❶ Halve the tomatoes and squeeze out the seeds and pulp. Put the flesh in the food processor with the onion and coriander and whiz until chopped.
❷ Transfer to a bowl and stir in the passata, beans and seasoning, plus 150 ml/$^1$/₄pint of cold water.
❸ Serve well chilled, with more coriander and tortilla chips.

make it your own You can use dry white wine instead of water in step 2. ● You can top the soup with a spoonful of homemade pesto: process a large handful of basil (or another herb) with 2 tbsp pine nuts, 25g/1oz Parmesan, 1 garlic clove and 3 tbsp olive oil. Add a splash of water if it is too thick to spoon.

per serving
Energy 92 kcalories, protein 5.1g, carbohydrate 16.8g, fat 1.0g, saturated fat 0.1g, fibre 3.7g, added sugars 1.3g, salt 0.56g ● Super-healthy; very low in calories and fat; good source of vitamin C; counts as 2 of your 5-a-day. Tomatoes (fresh, canned and cooked) are rich in lycopenes, which help prevent heart disease and cancer.

# fresh pea soup (simple)

**Serves 4 ● 10-20 minutes to prepare**

**This soup is deceptively simple, but never fails to surprise with its satisfying full flavour.  Frozen peas manage to keep a lot of their taste, but the fresh mint and chives make all the difference.**

**What you need**
450g / 1 lb frozen peas
generous handful of mint
4 tbsp double cream
a few chives

**Make sure you've got**
boiling water
good-quality vegetable bouillon powder,
    preferably Marigold (1 tbsp)

❶ Measure 850 ml / $1^1/_2$ pints of boiling water in a jug and add the bouillon powder and peas.
❷ Leave for at least 10 minutes, or until cool, then purée with the mint in a blender or processor until completely smooth. This will take a couple of minutes.
❸ Chill and serve with a swirl of cream and snipped chives on top.

**A liquidizer makes a smoother soup than a food processor.**

per serving **Energy 152 kcalories, protein 7.1g, carbohydrate 12.0g, fat 8.7g, saturated fat 4.9g, fibre 5.8g, added sugars none, salt 0.19g ● Super-healthy; low in saturated fat; counts as 1 of your 5-a-day.**

ABOVE chunky fresh tomato soup  RIGHT fresh pea soup

# panzanella *(simple)*

**Serves 2 ● 10-20 minutes to prepare (best left to sit for half an hour before eating)**

**The Tuscans don't like wasting bread, and when it begins to get stale, they use it in a sort of thick tomato soup (*pappa*) and this Tuscan bread salad.**

**What you need**
125g/4oz cucumber (about 9-10cm/3½-4in)
1 small red onion, very thinly sliced, or
    2 spring onions, shredded
12–15 cherry tomatoes, halved
1 packet of basil, leaves only
85g/3oz day-old ciabatta (¼ loaf)

**Make sure you've got**
extra-virgin olive oil (3 tbsp)
red wine vinegar (1 tbsp)

❶ Partly peel the cucumber with a potato peeler so it is striped. Slice down the centre and scrape out seeds and pulp. Cut across into thin slices and put in a sieve or colander with the red onion or spring onions. Sprinkle with 1 tsp salt and mix. Leave to drain.

❷ Squeeze the seeds and pulp out of the tomatoes and discard. Put the tomatoes in a serving bowl with the basil.

❸ Tear the bread (crusts and all) into bite-sized chunks and put them into a bowl of water. Immediately lift out handfuls and squeeze them dry (not so hard they are squashed, but enough that they are spongy) and transfer to the bowl with the tomatoes. Mix together and leave for about half an hour.

❹ Pat the cucumber and onion dry on paper towel and mix with the bread and tomato.
❺ Whisk the oil and vinegar to make a dressing and toss together with the salad. The salad should not need extra salt.

Dissertations have been written on what bread to use for panzanella, how stale it should be, exactly how hard to squeeze it out. I think, though, that the important thing is to use coarse country bread, and aim for the finished effect to be damp, light and fluffy.

make it your own This is meant to be a simple salad, but Tuscans sometimes add sliced anchovy fillets or chargrilled peppers, cut in strips, with the tomatoes. I like to add sliced mozzarella at the end.

per serving Energy 257 kcalories, protein 3.6g, carbohydrate 21.1g, fat 17.8g, saturated fat 2.6g, fibre 1.8g, added sugars none, salt 0.71g ● Super-healthy; low in saturated fat; counts as 1 of your 5-a-day.

panzanella

# prawn and avocado escabèche

**Serves 2 ● 10-15 minutes to prepare (start the day before, if convenient)**

An escabèche is a cold dish of cooked fish in a sweet-and-sour marinade, often involving chilli and vinegar – or, as here, lime juice.

**What you need**
juice of 1 lime
4 spring onions, shredded
200g/7oz cherry or plum tomatoes, pulp
    and seeds discarded, chopped
125g/4oz peeled cooked prawns, defrosted
    if frozen
1 ripe avocado, peeled, stoned and cubed
small handful of chopped coriander

**to serve**
1 Little Gem lettuce
ready-cooked poppadums

**Make sure you've got**
tomato purée (2 tsp)
pinch of dried oregano
1 green chilli, deseeded and finely chopped

❶ Mix the lime juice, spring onions, tomato purée, oregano, tomatoes and chilli in a non-metallic bowl. (You can refrigerate this marinade, covered with cling film, for up to 3 days.)
❷ Mix in the prawns, avocado and coriander, and leave for at least 10 minutes and up to 1 hour for the flavours to mingle.
❸ Arrange the lettuce leaves on plates and spoon the escabèche into the leaves. Serve accompanied with poppadums.

## make it your own Use another cooked fish, such as salmon; allow a slightly larger quantity and flake it in.

## per serving Energy 218 kcalories, protein 16.7g, carbohydrate 5.1g, fat 14.7g, saturated fat 1.7g, fibre 3.6g, added sugars none, salt 1.32g ● Super-healthy; low in saturated fat; counts as 2 of your 5-a-day.

# smoked mackerel and horseradish salad

**Per person ● 5-10 minutes to prepare**

**The pungency of horseradish is a classic foil for the oiliness of mackerel. The potato crisps give the salad a welcome crunch.**

**What you need**

1 smoked mackerel fillet (about 85g/3oz)

125g/4oz crisp lettuce

1 spring onion, shredded

1 ripe tomato, quartered, seeds and pulp
    discarded, then sliced

handful of potato crisps

**Make sure you've got**

grated horseradish or horseradish sauce ($^1/_2$ tsp)

white wine vinegar (1 tsp)

olive or sunflower oil (1 tbsp)

❶ Make the dressing by whisking together the horseradish, vinegar and oil.

❷ Flake the fish and shred the lettuce into a bowl. Scatter over the spring onion and tomato.

❸ Season the salad lightly (if the mackerel is peppered, you may need none at all) and toss in the dressing. Scatter over the crisps and enjoy.

## make it your own This is also good made with smoked trout fillets, or the new flaky hot-smoked salmon you can buy. In this case, use mustard instead of the horseradish.

## per serving Energy 485 kcalories, protein 18.2g, carbohydrate 10.0g, fat 41.6g, saturated fat 9.2g, fibre 2.2g, added sugars none, salt 1.92g ● Good source of omega-3 fatty acids, folic acid and vitamin C; counts as 2 of your 5-a-day.

# Thai prawns with lime noodles

**Serves 4 ● 15-20 minutes to prepare (stays good for 24 hours)**

**Although this is not authentically Oriental, it is very easy and low in fat.**

**What you need**
200g/7oz sugar snap peas, halved at an angle
200g/7oz peeled prawns, defrosted if frozen
195g tin of sweetcorn kernels, drained
4 spring onions, shredded
handful of coriander, chopped
2 limes, finely grated zest and juice of 1, the
    other cut into 4 wedges to serve

**Make sure you've got**
boiling water
flat rice noodles (rice sticks) (150g/5oz)
Thai sweet chilli sauce ( 1tbsp)
fish sauce (nam pla) (1 tbsp)

❶ Put the sugar snap peas in a bowl with a little salt, pour over boiling water and leave for 5 minutes to blanch. Drain.
❷ Do the same with the noodles.
❸ Meanwhile, mix the prawns, sweetcorn and spring onions in a serving bowl.
❹ Whisk the sauces with the lime zest and juice and add to the bowl along with the drained noodles.
❺ Stir in the coriander and serve with lime quarters.

**Flat rice noodles are so easy – put on the timer so you don't forget about them.**

make it your own **You can use 150g/5oz frozen peas instead of the sugar snaps – blanch them in exactly the same way.**

per serving **Energy 246 kcalories, protein 16.5g, carbohydrate 45.1g, fat 1.2, saturated fat 0.2g, fibre 1.5g, added sugars 3.2g, salt 2.24g ● Very low in fat and saturated fat; counts as 1 of your 5-a-day.**

# tuna and cannellini bean salad (simple)

**Serves 4 ● 10 minutes to prepare**

**What you need**
400g can of cannellini beans, rinsed and
    drained
small handful of mint, freshly chopped

**Make sure you've got**
150g can of tuna in oil, drained and flaked
1 small red onion, chopped
juice of ½ lemon

❶ Simply mix together all the ingredients and eat.

**per serving** Energy 130 kcalories, protein 13.3g, carbohydrate 12.5g, fat 3.4g, saturated fat 0.5g, fibre 3.5g, added sugars none, salt 0.39g ● Super-healthy; low in calories, fat and saturated fat; counts as 1 of your 5-a-day.

# tomato and prawn salad (simple)

**per person ● 10 minutes to prepare**

**What you need**
125g/4oz peeled cooked king prawns
1 large tomato, seeds and pulps discarded,
    sliced into pieces the same size as the
    prawns
chopped fresh coriander

**Make sure you've got**
flat rice noodles (rice sticks) (45g/1½oz)
boiling water
olive oil (1 tbsp)

❶ Snap the noodles in three, put into a bowl and pour boiling water over them. Add 1 tsp of salt and leave for 4 minutes.
❷ Meanwhile, mix together all the other ingredients in a bowl.
❸ Drain the noodles, stir into the contents of the bowl and eat.

**per serving** Energy 352 kcalories, protein 27.5g, carbohydrate 29.8g, fat 14.4g, saturated fat 1.7g, fibre 2.0g, added sugars none, salt 2.06g ● Low in saturated fat; good source of vitamin C; counts as 1 of your 5-a-day.

# trio of salsas

These classic Latin condiments make great accompaniments to bread, cheese, meat or fish, adding kick, freshness and lots of vitamins. The possibilities are endless, but your main ingredients should be diced rather than sliced, the consistency should be quite sloppy – and a salsa needs plenty of onion. Always mix them in a non-metal bowl (to avoid a metallic taint) and chill well. Literally 'raw sauce', salsa cruda is an excellent all-purpose juicy and chunky salsa, enough to serve with bread as a starter. For salsa verde, 'green salsa', cut everything fairly finely to make a sort of relish that is especially useful in cooling down hot dishes, or to serve with fish. Sweet, juicy, crunchy salsa rosso is great with meats and barbecues.

## salsa cruda (simple)

Serves 6 (can be halved) ● 10 minutes to prepare

**What you need**

2 orange, yellow or red peppers, deseeded
    and roughly chopped

6 small tomatoes, halved, seeds and pulp
    discarded, coarsely chopped

2 avocados, peeled, stoned and roughly
    chopped

small handful of coriander, chopped

**Make sure you've got**

1 small red onion, shredded

1 red or green chilli, deseeded and finely
    chopped

1 garlic clove, crushed (optional)

juice of $1/2$ lemon

❶ Mix everything except the avocado, lemon juice and coriander. Season and chill for up to 4 hours, until ready to eat.

❷ Prepare the avocado and fold it in. Squeeze over the lemon juice, scatter over the coriander and serve.

## per serving
Energy 114 kcalories, protein 2.0g, carbohydrate 6.0g, fat 9.4g, saturated fat 1.1g, fibre 3.1g, added sugars none, salt 0.03g ● Super-healthy; low in calories, saturated fat and salt; good source of vitamin C; counts as 2 of your 5-a-day.

# salsa verde *(simple)*

**Serves 4 ● 10 minutes to prepare**

**What you need**

2 spring onions, shredded

1 green pepper, deseeded and roughly chopped

5 cm/2 in cucumber, unpeeled, deseeded and diced

1 green chilli, deseeded and finely chopped

zest and juice of $\frac{1}{2}$ lime

small handful of coriander or mint, chopped

**Make sure you've got**

1 garlic clove, optional)

extra-virgin olive oil (2 tbsp)

sugar ($\frac{1}{4}$ tsp)

capers (1 tsp, rinsed and chopped)

❶ Up to 4 hours ahead, mix together everything except the herbs, and season. Chill.

❷ Toss lightly again and serve.

per serving Energy 61 kcalories, protein 0.7g, carbohydrate 2.0g, fat 5.7g, saturated fat 0.8g, fibre 0.9g, added sugars 0.3g, salt 0.03g ● **Super-healthy; low in calories, fat, saturated fat and salt; good source of vitamin C.**

# salsa rosso *(simple)*

**Serves 4 ● 10 minutes to prepare**

**What you need**

1 small red onion, shredded

4 medium tomatoes, halved, seeds and pulp
   discarded, coarsely chopped

1 red pepper, deseeded and coarsely chopped
   (preferably tapered romano peppers)

8 radishes, trimmed and roughly chopped

few sprigs of purple (or green) basil

**Make sure you've got**

extra-virgin olive oil (2 tbsp)

1 orange, peeled and cut into small
   pieces

❶ Up to 4 hours ahead, mix together everything except the basil. Season and chill.

❷ Toss lightly again and scatter with the basil.

per serving Energy 97 kcalories, protein 1.7g, carbohydrate 9.7g, fat 6.0g, saturated fat 0.8g, fibre 2.4g, added sugars none, salt 0.03g ● **Super-healthy; very low in calories, saturated fat and salt; good source of vitamin C; counts as 2 of your 5-a-day.**

# fruit fancies

Fruit is obviously one of the greatest allies of the no-cook. Good ripe fruit in season will always satisfy – and look good – with little or nothing needing to be done to it. Here, though, are some simple but effective ways with fruit that will help bring out its best qualities – a little honey here to amplify sweetness, some nuts or a little cheese there to provide a contrast in texture, alcohol and/or spices for added zing generally.

1 cherries with ricotta Put cherries and ricotta on a platter, top with some honey and help yourselves. Grapes are also good this way – especially black seedless.

2 cardamom and orange-flavoured fruits Slice fruits of the season and drizzle them lightly with Grand Marnier and a pinch of ground cardamom.

3 fruity yoghurt Slice fresh apricots or peaches and cover with yoghurt into which you have stirred a little fine-cut marmalade.

4 raspberry ripple Mix fresh or defrosted raspberries with Quark until it is streaked and pink. Drizzle with a little honey to serve.

5 summer fruit delight Slice peaches or other summer fruits into a dish and drizzle with a little orange juice or liqueur. Crumble over some amaretti biscuits and leave for a few minutes before eating.

**6** fruit salsa Make a fruit salsa to serve with or after spicy food by chopping a small onion and adding the juice of 2 limes. Chop the flesh of a mango (or pawpaw, small pineapple, or 2 peaches), a small red pepper and plenty of coriander. Mix, season and splash with orange juice. You can add a finely chopped chilli, if you wish.

**7** Les quatre mendicants Arrange on a plate some fresh figs dusted in icing sugar, walnut halves, juicy raisins and macadamia nuts or almonds. The name refers to four monastic orders – Franciscan (grey habits), Augustinian (brown), Dominican (black), and Carmelite (white).

**8** nut-stuffed dates Remove the stones from juicy fresh dates and replace with a mixture of chopped pistachios, pine kernels and honey. Anoint them with rosewater just before serving.

**9** banana salad Slice some bananas, drizzle them with lemon or lime juice and honey, and sprinkle over a handful of chopped dates and walnuts. Serve with a dollop of fromage frais.

**10** peach and cherry refresher Mix peaches and stoned cherries, and pour over a little orange flower water mixed with vodka or schnapps.

fruit salsa

**Les quatre mendicants**

nut-stuffed dates

banana salad

bought desserts are all well and good, but some of the most sumptuous and creative last courses of all require no more effort than melting chocolate and mixing in a few luxurious extras, or glitzing up some bought ice-cream

# dashing desserts

# fresh raspberry truffles

**Makes 20-24 small truffles ● 20 minutes to prepare, plus cooling**

**This makes a very soft, fresh-tasting truffle. You need a light touch – if you are the impatient sort, just don't attempt this.**

**What you need**
150g/5oz fresh or defrosted frozen
    raspberries
125g/4oz best dark chocolate
4 tbsp double cream

**Make sure you've got**
butter (15g/½oz)
maple syrup, honey or golden syrup (2 tsp)
cocoa powder (15g/½oz), sifted

❶ Whiz the raspberries in a food processor for 30 seconds, until completely liquid. Put into a sieve and use a spatula or wooden spoon to squeeze the liquid through into a medium bowl, leaving the seeds behind. Discard the seeds. This sounds a bother, but is actually the work of 3-4 minutes, and I use it as an opportunity to marvel at the stupendous bright pink raspberry colour as I do so.

❷ Break the chocolate into the bowl and add the cream, butter and syrup or honey. Heat in the microwave or over hot water, stirring frequently, until the chocolate has melted and the mixture is smooth and glossy. In my 600w microwave, it takes about 1 minute to get the mixture hot, then I stir until the chocolate is fully melted.

❸ Stir the sieved raspberry purée into the melted chocolate until completely mixed. Let cool and then refrigerate overnight, or until the mixture does not stick to your finger when pressed.

❹ Now comes the messy (fun) bit. Put the cocoa into a shallow bowl. Scoop a generous teaspoon of the mixture into your hands and roll it into a ball. Drop in the cocoa. Repeat for 4 more balls. Roll the balls about in the cocoa with a spoon and lift on to a plate lined with a piece of baking paper. Repeat with the rest of the mixture to make 20-24 truffles. Keep chilled, serve straight from the fridge and eat within a week.

**It may sound kinky, but you can use a pair of surgical gloves in step 4 to roll and dust the truffles.**

# after-dinner Lamingtons

**Makes 30 mini-Lamingtons (allow 1 or 2 each, but they will all get eaten regardless) ● 1 hour to prepare (put on the radio and lose yourself; best made a couple of hours ahead, although they keep for a couple of days in a tin)**

**Thrill an Aussie by serving chic bite-sizes of their national tea-time favourite with after-dinner coffee.**

**What you need**
400g/14oz bought Madeira cake, preferably
    square or rectangular
150g/5oz golden icing sugar
150g/5oz desiccated coconut
1 tbsp raspberry jam
1 tbsp redcurrant jelly

**Make sure you've got**
melted butter (3 tbsp)
boiling water (3 tbsp)
cocoa (1 tbsp)
2 tbsp juice and finely grated zest of $\frac{1}{2}$
    lemon

❶ Trim any brown parts off the cake and slice it as neatly as possible into thirty 2.5cm/1in squares. Assemble a production line. Put the cake squares on a plate, then set out a bowl for the icing plus a larger bowl for it to sit in, a bowl for the coconut and 3 plates, each covered with baking paper. You will need 2 forks for dipping in the icing, and two more forks for turning in the coconut.

❷ Make the chocolate icing by mixing the 1 tbsp of the melted butter, 1 tbsp boiling water, the cocoa and one-third of the golden icing sugar. Thin to a coating consistency with another teaspoon of boiling water if necessary.

❸ Tip a third of the coconut into the coconut bowl. One by one, put one-third of the squares in the chocolate icing and cover all over using the forks. Allow excess icing to drip off, then drop the square in the coconut. Use the other forks to roll it all over in coconut, then transfer to the paper-lined plate.

❹ The icing will begin to set – when this happens, put boiling water in the bowl beneath the icing, or towards the end you can add a tsp of boiling water.

❺ Repeat with half the remaining cake squares and raspberry icing made in the same way as the chocolate but replacing the cocoa with the raspberry jam and redcurrant jelly, and then with the rest of the cake squares and the lemon icing again made in the same way, replacing the cocoa with the finely grated zest and 2 tbsp of juice from the lemon, washing up the icing and dipping stations, and replenishing the coconut bowl in between.

# peach tea jelly

**Serves 4-6 ● 10-20 minutes to prepare (make a day ahead)**

**What you need**
2 tbsp orange liqueur, such as Curaçao or
    Grand Marnier
about 350 ml/12 fl oz Tazo peach tea
    (see below)
fortune cookies, to serve

**Make sure you've got**
sugar (4 tsp)
12g sachet of gelatine
boiling water
juice of 1 lemon
juice of 1 orange

❶ Mix the sugar and gelatine in a cup. Pour 50 ml/2 fl oz boiling water into a measuring jug, sprinkle on the gelatine and sugar and stir to dissolve.
❷ When completely dissolved, add the fruit juices and liqueur and top up to about 600 ml/1 pint with the peach tea. Stir well to ensure no solid bits of gelatine remain.
❸ Strain into wine glasses and chill to set.
❹ Serve with fortune cookies to complete the eastern feel.

Tazo is a delicious green tea flavoured with herbs and spices; you can use any other tea, but it needs to be strong and sweet ● There is a lot of nonsense talked about gelatine, but it is nothing to be scared of. Make sure it has dissolved and strain before use, in case a lump or particle has escaped your notice, and you can't go wrong.

make it your own For sheer elegance, try fresh orange jelly, made in the same way. Dissolve the gelatine and 4 tbsp sugar in 3 tbsp boiling water, then add the finely grated zest of 1 orange, the juice of 4, the juice of 1 lemon and 2 tbsp orange liqueur. Make up to 600 ml/1 pint, if necessary, with more juice or water. Pour into glasses (don't strain - it tastes fresher). With this formula (1 sachet of powdered gelatine to 600 ml/1 pint of liquid) you can set almost anything you can think of – coffee, smoothies, juices – you name it. Three things to remember:
❶ The mixture you're setting needs to be well sweetened.
❷ If you add liqueur or any other alcohol, the jelly will not set as firmly.
❸ If you own an elaborate jelly mould, say of Windsor Castle, and wish to use it, add 1 tsp extra gelatine to the mixture for a firmer set.

# strawberry-misu

**Serves 8 ● 20-30 minutes to prepare (make at least 4 hours, and up to a day, ahead)**

**What you need**

250g/9oz strawberries

250g tub of mascarpone

200g tub of fromage frais

1 small cup of espresso coffee (or 85ml/3fl oz
   strong black coffee)

150g/5oz savoiardi biscuits, or sponge fingers

**Make sure you've got**

2 egg yolks

golden caster sugar (4 tbsp)

4 tbsp brandy or kirsch

4 tbsp Marsala

cocoa powder, for dusting

❶ Beat the egg yolks with 2 tbsp sugar until pale and creamy - this takes a full 5 minutes by hand, 3 minutes with an electric whisk and 2 minutes in a standing mixer or processor (if your processor is equipped with a small bowl).

❷ Mix the brandy or kirsch and the Marsala. Put the coffee in a small wide bowl and stir in half the Marsala mix.

❸ Meanwhile, put the strawberries in a jug with the remaining sugar and mash. Mix the mascarpone and fromage frais, then beat in the egg yolk and the remaining Marsala mix until creamy.

❹ If you wish to make the strawberry-misu directly on a serving plate, stand the ring from a 20cm/8in springform cake tin in its centre; otherwise use the tin in the usual fashion. Dip the biscuits very briefly in the coffee mix (don't let them get soggy) and use to layer the bottom of the tin completely, cutting to shape as necessary.

❺ Spoon over half the mascarpone mix to cover the biscuits completely. Sift over a thick dusting of cocoa. Repeat with another layer of dunked biscuits, as before, then spoon the strawberries over evenly, followed by the remaining mascarpone. Finally, dust over more cocoa and leave in the fridge to set. Serve cut into wedges.

**If the cocoa has melted into the topping, sift over a fresh layer just before serving.**

## make it your own **This is also gorgeous with raspberries. ● If serving larger numbers, make the same size of dessert but serve smaller portions, accompanied with extra fruit.**

strawberry-misu

# red fruits in a rose blanket *(simple)*

**Serves 8 ● 10-20 minutes to prepare**

**What you need**
225g/8oz fresh strawberries
175g/6oz fresh raspberries
125g/4oz redcurrants or blackcurrants
1 tbsp rosewater
1 tbsp orange flower water

**for the rose cream**
1 egg white
142ml carton of double cream
1 dsp rosewater
1 dsp orange flower water
petals of a small well-scented rose, to strew

**Make sure you've got**
caster sugar (2 tbsp)
icing sugar (2 tbsp)

## ahead
❶ Hull the strawberries and halve them. Pick over the raspberries and pick the currants off their stems. Arrange in one layer in a large shallow dish, with the cut sides of the strawberries facing up. Sprinkle with the caster sugar and the flower waters and leave for up to 2 hours.

## at the last minute
❷ Whip the egg white until it begins to stiffen and whisk in 1 tbsp icing sugar. Beat until stiff but not dry. Using the same whisk or beaters but in another bowl, whip the cream until it is stiff, adding the remaining 1 tbsp icing sugar and the remaining 2 dsp flower waters. Fold in the egg white.
❸ Spoon gently over the fruits and serve scattered with rose petals.

You can crystallize rose petals by brushing them with egg white and dredging them in caster sugar. Leave to dry on a wire rack for 4 hours. You can make these a day ahead and keep in a tin; otherwise use the petals as they are.

## make it your own I love the simplicity of this dessert, but if you would like to build it into something more impressive, make individual rose meringues. Put individual meringues on plates, top with the fruit and juices, then cover generously with cream. You'll have enough for 10–12.

# mango and lime fool (simple)

**Serves 4 (easily halved or doubled)  ● 15-25 minutes to prepare (make ahead)**

**This fool is the palest apricot colour, flecked with lime zest.**

**What you need**

1 large ripe mango (or 250g/9oz prepared
    mango)
finely grated zest of 1 lime
1 tbsp Curaçao or other orange liqueur
100ml/3½ fl oz fresh ready-made custard
284ml carton of double cream

**Make sure you've got**

golden caster sugar (2-3 tbsp)

## ahead

❶ Liquidize the mango with most of the lime zest (you'll need to grate a little extra
when serving) and liqueur until smooth. Add the custard and sugar, and whiz the
mixture again.

❷ In a big bowl, whip the cream until stiff. Pour in the mango and custard mixture.
Use your whisk gently to combine everything until no longer streaky.

❸ Taste for sweetness – mangoes vary – and add the extra sugar if it needs it.
Transfer to small glasses and chill for at least 3 hours, but preferably 24 hours.

## at the last minute

❹ Grate over a little extra lime zest – if you have a Microplane grater or, better still,
a zester, so much the prettier – and taste the tropics.

## make it your own Add orange flower water instead of liqueur for a more fragrant
dessert, or rum for something more tropical.

# blackberry mascarpone shortbread

**Serves 4 (easily multiplied)**  ● **15 minutes to prepare**

**What you need**
125g/4oz shortbread biscuits (6 biscuits)
150g/5oz mascarpone
150g/5oz fresh blackberries

**Make sure you've got**
butter (25g/1oz)
honey (2 tsp)
icing sugar, to sift over

❶ Make a shortbread base by melting the butter in the microwave (covered with cling film in case it sputters) or a pan and whizzing it with the biscuits in a processor. Tip the buttery crumbs on to a flat plate or the rimless base of a tart tin and freeze for 15 minutes. Once firm enough to handle, transfer to a serving plate and keep chilled.
❷ Just before serving, mix the mascarpone gently with the honey (far easier at room temperature), but don't overdo it or it will curdle, and spread over the shortbread.
❸ Arrange the blackberries over the top. Dust with icing sugar and serve cut in wedges.

## make it your own This is also good with strawberries, raspberries, blueberries or a mixture.

Even easier, use one bought shortbread biscuit about 6-7cm/2$^1$/$_2$-3in in diameter per person. Anchor on a serving plate by dabbing a little honey in the centre. For each, mix 2 tbsp mascarpone with $^1$/$_2$ tsp honey, spread on the biscuit, pile on 85g/3oz fruit and dust with icing sugar as above.

# white chocolate and summer fruit pashka

**Serves 6 ● 15-20 minutes to prepare (make at least 2 hours, or up to a day, ahead)**

**What you need**

100g bar of white chocolate, melted

150g/5oz cottage cheese

125g/4oz light cream cheese

125g/4oz crème fraîche

125g/4oz mixed glacé or dried fruits (organic
    dried apricots, raisins, cherries), chopped

25g/1oz walnuts, chopped

325g/11oz fresh raspberries, hulled
    strawberries or cherries

**Make sure you've got**

vanilla extract (1 tsp)

❶ Melt the white chocolate, either over a bowl of hot water or in the microwave on low for about a minute, stirring at half-time.

❷ Put the cheeses and crème fraîche in a processor and blitz for a good minute until smooth. Add the white chocolate and vanilla.

❸ Transfer to a bowl and stir in the glacé or dried fruits and the nuts. With a piece of muslin about 30cm/12inch square or a new J-cloth that has been rinsed and squeezed out, line a 600ml/1pint bowl or mould so it overhangs the top. Pile in the mixture.

❹ Leave to set in the fridge for at least 2 hours. When ready to serve, fold back the cloth, invert the pashka on to a dish and remove the cloth completely. Serve the pashka in spoonfuls with the soft fruits.

In the traditional recipe, the pashka is left to drain (hence the cheesecloth). In this recipe this is not necessary, but the cloth is used to give the surface of the dessert its characteristically pretty texture.

make it your own If you have 6 small dariole moulds or coffee cups, you can make individual pashkas. Line them as above, turn out into the centre of plates and serve surrounded by the fruits.

# the ultimate chocolate fridge cake

**Cuts into 12-15 rich pieces ● 20-30 minutes to prepare**

**What you need**

125g/4oz seedless raisins

4 organic dried apricots, chopped (if you enjoy
measuring, that's 25g/1oz)

200g/7oz dark chocolate (go for 70% cocoa
solids)

125g/4oz sweetened chestnut purée

125g/4oz digestive biscuits (8 biscuits),
roughly broken

50g/2oz toasted hazelnuts or toasted flaked
almonds, chopped

**Make sure you've got**

finely grated zest of $^1/_2$ orange

4 tbsp brandy

butter (125g/4oz)

cocoa (1 tbsp)

icing sugar, for dusting

## ahead

❶ Soak the raisins, apricots and orange zest in the brandy – you can do this while
you melt the chocolate, or up to a day in advance.

❷ In the microwave or over hot water, melt the chocolate, butter and cocoa in a large
bowl. Meanwhile, line a 18cm/7in square tin, or 450g/1lb loaf tin with foil.

❸ Stir the chocolate mixture until smooth and then stir in the raisin-brandy mixture
and chestnut purée, and break in the biscuits roughly with the nuts. When all is
glistening and well coated, transfer to your prepared tin (if using a loaf tin, it will fill it
to the brim), smooth the top carefully and put in the fridge.

## at the last minute

❹ Cut the cake into fingers, dust with icing sugar and stack up appealingly to serve.
If making in a loaf tin, remove from the tin, dust with sugar and serve cut in slices.

Many recipes include an egg to stop this setting like a rock, but chestnut purée has the same
effect and adds its luxurious flavour. ● Organic dried apricots have an richer, fruitier flavour.

## make it your own You can ritz this up with chopped pistachio nuts, glacé fruits of your
choice and even sliced marrons glacés. ● Instead of brandy, try kirsch, whisky or rum.

# chocolate muffin trifles *(simple)*

**Serves 4 ● 10-20 minutes to prepare**

**What you need**

3 chocolate muffins

142 ml carton of whipping cream

5 tbsp Tia Maria or amaretto, plus more for
   sprinkling

250g tub of mascarpone

**Make sure you've got**

dark chocolate (150g/5oz), melted

## ahead

❶ Have ready 4 large wine glasses. Crumble the muffins lightly into a bowl. Melt the chocolate over hot water or in the microwave and leave to cool slightly.

❷ Whip the cream until stiff, adding the 5 tbsp liqueur towards the end. If using an electric whisk, use it to beat the mascarpone until softened. Now combine the cream and mascarpone, using the whisk in a cutting action, or the beaters of the electric whisk, not actually turning.

❸ Pour the cooled chocolate over and lightly fold together until rippled - stop before you think you're done, as you want a strong effect.

❹ Divide half the muffin crumble between the wine glasses. Sprinkle each lightly with some of the liqueur.

❺ Spoon or pour over half the chocolate mix. Then repeat the layers.

## make it your own Use a potato peeler to flick over chocolate curls.

# kirsch ice cream cake *(simple)*

**Serves 6-8 ● 10-20 minutes to prepare**

**This recipe is based on a dessert created many years ago by a London hotel in honour of a long-forgotten royal wedding. I served a version of it when I appeared on *Masterchef*. It is unusual and sophisticated.**

**What you need**
450ml/¾pint double cream, or a mixture of
    double cream and crème fraîche
3 tbsp kirsch or vodka
6-8 ready made meringues (about 85g/3oz),
    broken up

**Make sure you've got**
finely grated zest of 1 lemon
4 knobs of stem ginger, finely chopped

## ahead
❶ Line a shallow 18cm/7inch cake tin with cling film.
❷ Whip the cream until just stiff and fold in the remaining ingredients, including the meringues (it's tidiest to break them up while still in the wrapper - aim for pieces no bigger than a walnut). Pile into the tin and smooth the top.
❸ Freeze for 4 hours or longer.

## at the last minute
❹ About 10 minutes before serving, turn out on a serving plate, remove the cling film and serve cut in wedges.

This is a very rich and exciting dessert, best served with sharp fruits such as physalis, strawberries or raspberries, or pineapple or orange in winter. Alternatively, serve with a fruit coulis.

# frozen assets

**Test whether ice cream is too hard or ready to serve with a thin skewer. About 15-30 minutes in the fridge gives most ices time to soften; this is far easier than doing battle with a brick-like block of ice and bending your best spoon into the bargain. If you're in a hurry, microwave in bursts.**

**1** instant warm chocolate sauce Heat 150 ml / ¼ pint single cream with 1 tbsp golden caster sugar and a knob of butter until boiling. Whiz 100g/3½oz dark chocolate in a processor and pour in the cream. Process until smooth and add a few drops of vanilla extract, brandy or rum. Great with vanilla, butterscotch or chocolate ice cream.

**2** hot espresso sauce Make 175 ml / 6 fl oz very strong coffee. While still very hot, whisk in 200g/7oz dark chocolate, finely chopped, and 50g/2oz butter. Great with coffee, chocolate or vanilla ice cream.

**3** ice cream pie Make the crumb crust on page 153 and freeze it in its tin. Allow 850 ml - 1 litre / 1½ - 1¾ pints of ice cream to soften just enough to make it easy to spoon, and pack half into the crust. Top the layer of ice cream with a few handfuls of crushed bourbon biscuits or sliced Mars Bars, then spread over the rest of the ice cream. Freeze again and top with more biscuits or chocolate nuts to serve.

**4** butterscotch ripple ice cream Stir dulce de leche (also known as banoffee pie filling) into softened vanilla ice cream until streaky. Serve at once with a warm or hot sauce. You can warm dulce de leche in the microwave to make an instant butterscotch sauce.

**5** ice cream surprise By the same principle, you can stir any or several of the following into softened vanilla ice cream: chocolate espresso beans, chopped mint chocolate, chopped Toblerone, chopped chocolate biscuits, chopped marshmallows, Smarties (though the colour runs a bit alarmingly). If you want to do this ahead, go for softer scoop ice cream, and don't let it melt too far before refreezing.

**6** ice cream sandwiches Make ice cream sandwiches by freezing two large thin biscuits per person. When frozen, sandwich with just-softened ice cream, press chopped chocolate or nuts round the sides and refreeze again until hard, wrapping each sandwich tightly in cling film. This is a great individual dessert to keep for when you deserve a treat.

**7** sprinkle toppings Add some sparkle with ice cream sprinkles. After scooping, sprinkle with chocolate nuts and raisins, jelly beans, crushed biscuits, miniature marshmallows or chopped chocolates (After Eights or truffles!).

**8** Italian affogato For Italian affogato, put a scoop of vanilla ice cream in a heatproof dish or glass and pour over a small, very strong hot espresso.

**9** fruit coulis Make raspberry, strawberry or blueberry coulis by blending 250g/9oz fresh or defrosted berries with the juice of ½ lemon. If using raspberries, press through a sieve with a spatula or wooden spoon, frequently scraping the underside, which speeds things up. Stir in sugar to taste – about 3tbsp. Strawberry coulis can be a bit pale, so add a handful of raspberries if you wish, plus extra lemon juice to sharpen. Blueberry coulis may start to set, so thin with water if necessary. Serve with fruit ice creams or vanilla.

**10** Grand Marnier fruits Keep a jar to drizzle over vanilla ice cream. Chop a mixture of glacé and dried fruits - cherries, ginger, peel, raisins, dried apricots (good for using up the ends of packets) - and put in a jar. Cover with Grand Marnier, Cointreau or brandy and leave in the fridge for at least a week and up to two months. (Also great drizzled between layers of a bread and butter pudding.)

fruit coulis

ice cream sandwiches

sprinkle toppings

Italian affogato

# mocha hedgehog (simple)

**Serves 6** ● **15-25 minutes to prepare (make a day in advance or freeze, up to the end of step 3)**

**This is grand and impressive, but astonishingly simple to make.**

**What you need**
85g/3oz ground almonds
125g/4oz Rich Tea biscuits (about15 biscuits)

**for the finishing touch**
50g/2oz whole toasted almonds, or 25g/1oz
    flaked toasted almonds
142ml carton of double or whipping cream
coffee liqueur (1 tbsp)

**Make sure you've got**
strong black coffee (200ml/7fl oz)
unsalted butter (85g/3oz)
golden caster sugar (1 tbsp)

## ahead
❶ Make the coffee (the easiest way is to filter it into a large measuring bowl) and, while still hot, add the butter and sugar. Stir until melted, then stir in the ground almonds. Break in the biscuits and leave for about 10 minutes, until beginning to thicken.
❷ Line a 600ml/1pint bowl with cling film. Pour in the biscuit mixture and flatten the top. Refrigerate overnight. If using whole toasted almonds, split them in two down the centre.

## shortly before serving
❸ Whip the cream until stiff and, as it thickens, whip in the liqueur until stiff. Unmould the pudding on to a plate, peel off the cling film and spoon over the cream. Stick the nuts all over, hedgehog-fashion.

# cantuccini log (simple)

**Serves 6** ● **20-30 minutes to prepare**

**This is a grown up variation of the choc-chip log many of us made as children.**

**What you need**
150 g / 5 oz cantuccini biscuits (20 small
  biscuits)
100 ml / 3½ fl oz whipping cream
100 ml / 3½ fl oz double cream
chocolate, to grate on top

**Make sure you've got**
finely grated zest and juice of 1 orange
orange liqueur (2 tbsp)
allspice (½ tsp)

## ahead
❶ Practise the shape by laying down a row of 10 cantuccini biscuits upright with another 10 on top of them in a second layer. Choose your serving plate.
❷ Whisk the orange zest and juice with half the liqueur. Whip the creams to soft peaks with the allspice and remaining liqueur.
❸ Dip a biscuit first in the orange mixture, then put a spoonful of cream on top and stand the biscuit as it was first time round. Continue until you have your bottom layer. Spoon a little cream on top then continue with second layer.
❹ If you have any orange mixture left, fold it into remaining cream, then spread the cream over the log and drag a fork across to make an attractive pattern.
❺ Refrigerate for a couple of hours or overnight.

## at the last minute
❻ Sprinkle with grated chocolate and serve cut in slices.

## Make it your own You can use flavoured or chocolate chip cantuccini. ● You can use ground cinnamon or nutmeg instead of the allspice if that's what you have.

# glossy choc-peanut butter cheesecake

**Serves 8 ● 20-30 minutes to prepare (make ahead)**

**If you're feeling indulgent, you may as well do the job properly. This cheesecake is the dessert equivalent of that trendy piece of American confectionery known as Reese's Pieces – only it's much nicer.**

**What you need for the crust**
200g/7oz digestive biscuits (about 14),
    put in a bag and finely crushed with a
    sledgehammer or rolling pin

**for the filling**
250g tub of cream cheese
150g/5oz peanut butter (smooth or chunky,
    as you wish)
284ml carton of double or whipping cream

**for the glossy topping**
50g/2oz dark chocolate, broken into pieces

**Make sure you've got**
butter (125g/4oz), melted
golden syrup (2 tbsp)
golden caster sugar (50g/2oz)
icing sugar (25g/1oz)

❶ Line a 20cm/8inch springform cake tin with baking paper. Put three-quarters of the butter and the syrup in a medium bowl and melt in the microwave or over hot water. Stir in the biscuits. Turn into the tin and, using your hands, press all over the base and slightly up the sides. Refrigerate while you make the filling.

❷ Put the cream cheese, peanut butter and golden caster sugar in a processor and whiz – the mixture will be heavy and sticky. Pour 175ml/6fl oz of the cream ($^2/_3$ of the carton) into the peanut butter mixture and process, scraping down sides as necessary. Spoon into the crust, smoothing the top carefully with a spatula to get it dead level.

❸ Put the remaining cream, butter, chocolate and icing sugar in a bowl and melt in the microwave or over hot water, then whisk till smooth and glossy. Pour on top of the peanut filling and chill for at least an hour or overnight.

# bitter chocolate torte

**Serves 8-10 ● 30-40 minutes to prepare (make at least 4 hours ahead)**

**This may look complex, but it's actually quite easy, intensely chocolaty and wonderfully alcoholic.**

**For the biscuit base**
50g/2oz dark chocolate
175g/6oz digestive biscuits (about 12 biscuits)

**For the bitter chocolate filling**
150g bar of dark chocolate

**For the topping**
284ml carton of double cream
cocoa powder or a few chocolate coffee beans

**Make sure you've got**
cocoa (2 tbsp)
butter (50g/2oz)
golden caster sugar (6 tbsp)
4 tbsp freshly brewed extra strong espresso or
    filter coffee
4 eggs, separated
vanilla extract (1 tsp)
brandy (4 tbsp)

## ahead

❶ Place the ring from an 20cm/8in springform cake tin upside down on a serving plate and line the edge with baking paper. To make the base, melt the chocolate with the cocoa and butter in a large bowl in a microwave or over hot water. Blitz the biscuits and 2 tbsp caster sugar in a processor until soft and crumbly – but don't continue until they turn to sand. Stir into the melted mixture, then pile into the lined tin. Use a spoon and your fingers to press the crumbs lightly up the sides, then over the base. You will need an interior depth of at least 4cm/1¹/₂in. Do not make the top too straight – a thinner and wavier edge is more attractive, while a straight one can vanish to nothing – and avoid a thick heel of crumbs in the corner. Put in the fridge to chill while you make the mousse.

❷ Make the filling: melt the chocolate in the coffee in a microwave or over hot water. Meanwhile, beat the egg yolks with the vanilla. Stir in the chocolate and, when smooth, the brandy.

❸ Beat 3 of the egg whites until almost stiff, then start beating in 3 tablespoons of sugar. Continue until the mixture forms peaks when you lift the beaters, and the peaks fall rather than stay upright. Fold into the chocolate mixture, then transfer to the chilled base. Chill for 4 hours or overnight.

## to finish
❹ Remove the springform ring and lining paper. Softly whip the cream with 1 tbsp sugar until just stiffening and billow over the filling. Dust with cocoa powder or decorate with chocolate coffee beans to serve.

**For the full-on chocolate effect, use 70% cocoa solids chocolate throughout.**

## make it your own
**You can flavour this torte with whisky or a liqueur rather than brandy. Bourbon or rum work beautifully, or amaretto or the hazelnut-flavoured Frangelico.**
● **Decorate it in your own style. Simply grate chocolate, or make chocolate curls. If using amaretto liqueur in the torte, go for toasted almonds or chocolate almonds; if Frangelico, go for hazelnuts.** ● **For an extra-bouffant topping, whisk a large egg white with 1 tablespoon golden caster sugar to the soft peak stage and fold into the cream.**

bitter chocolate torte

# the no-cook storecupboard, etc.

**The basics the no-cook
should have in**
(i.e. 'Make sure you've got's)

anchovy fillets
balsamic vinegar
*bananas
brandy
*bread (white)
capers
caraway seeds
cayenne
*chillies (fresh)
chutney
cider vinegar
coriander (ground)
cornichons
couscous
cumin
curry paste
*eggs
extra-virgin olive oil
fish sauce (nam pla)
*garlic
gelatine
*ginger (fresh)
good-quality bouillon powder,
    preferably Marigold
harissa paste
hoisin sauce
honey (clear)
horseradish
horseradish sauce
Japanese rice wine
maple syrup
marsala
mayonnaise

*milk
mustard (Dijon)
mustard (wholegrain)
nutmeg
olive oil
olives
*onions (yellow and red)
*oranges
oregano (dried)
paprika
peanut butter
pesto
pine nuts
red wine vinegar
rice noodles (instant)
rice wine vinegar
rosewater
sesame oil (toasted)
sherry (dry)
sherry vinegar
soy sauce
sugar, white
sugar, brown
sultanas or seedless raisins
sun-dried tomato (in oil)
sunflower oil
sunflower oil (toasted)
Tabasco sauce
Thai sweet chilli sauce
tomato ketchup
tomato purée or sun-dried
    tomato purée
tuna (canned)
vermicelli
walnut oil
white wine vinegar
Worcestershire sauce

**Other ingredients
invaluable to the no-cook**
(many of these are already in
the lists at the front of the
book)

argan oil
avruga (herring) caviar
basil
broad beans (young)
butter (unsalted)
cannellini beans (canned)
celery
chervil
chickpeas (canned)
chillies (crushed)
chives
cinnamon (ground)
coriander (fresh leaves)
crème fraîche
cucumber
custard
feta in oil
fromage frais
goats' cheese
ice cream
limes
mascarpone
mustard and cress
paprika
parsley
peas
poppy seeds
prawns
rocket
smoked salmon
smoked paprika
spring onions
tarragon
tomatoes
watercress

* non-storecupboard item (i.e. one for the fridge or freezer)

# index

## acknowledgements

My thanks to everyone who has inspired the recipes in this book, especially Henrietta Green for her generous sharing of ideas and expertise.

Since my schooldays, my sounding board on all matters culinary has been Stephen Mudge, now based in Paris. I would like to thank him for his benign influence over the years I have been cooking, and his suggestions for this book.

The team at BBC Good Food is a daily inspiration to work with, and I never stop learning from them – thanks especially to Mary Cadogan, Angela Nilsen, Sara Buenfeld, Barney Desmazery and Jeni Wright, as well as the unflappable Sarah Astell and nutritionist Dr Wendy Doyle, who prepared the nutritional analyses for my healthy eating chapter.

The philosophy of this book is that ingredients are everything: I would like to thank Thane Prince for opening my eyes to this at her Aldeburgh Cookery School, and Francesca Fabbri, who enlightened me on bruschetta and crostini.

At Quadrille Publishing, my thanks go to Alison Cathie, Jane O'Shea, Lewis Esson and Mary Evans for their talent and professionalism, also to Jason Lowe and Jane Suthering for their mouthwatering photographs.

Finally, for support and encouragement during the arduous weeks of recipe development and testing, Peter Steggall, Pat and Patsy Murrin, and Andrew Leonard.